FAITHFUL STEPS

May God bless your path as you walk closer with Him.

FAITHFUL STEPS

A closer walk with God

THOMAS A MAYBERRY

Thomas A Mayberry

© 2023 Thomas A Mayberry
All rights reserved. No portion of this book may be reproduced, stored in a retrieval system, or transmitted in any form or by any means – electronic, mechanical, photocopy, recording, scanning, or other – except for brief quotations in critical reviews or articles, without the prior written permission of the publisher.

Scripture references are from the following sources.

The ESV® Bible (The Holy Bible, English Standard Version®). ESV® Text Edition: 2016. Copyright © 2001 by Crossway, a publishing ministry of Good News Publishers.

THE HOLY BIBLE, NEW INTERNATIONAL VERSION®, NIV® Copyright © 1973, 1978, 1984, 2011 by Biblica, Inc.® Used by permission. All rights reserved worldwide.

Holy Bible, New Living Translation, copyright © 1996, 2004, 2015 by Tyndale House Foundation. Used by permission of Tyndale House Publishers, Inc., Carol Stream, Illinois 60188. All rights reserved.

This dedication is a heartfelt tribute to remind us of the power of family and the impact they have on shaping our lives. It is the essence of gratitude and the importance of passing down core values from one generation to another. It serves as a powerful reminder to cherish our loved ones and honor the foundations they have laid for us—a testament to the enduring legacy of family bonds and the values that shape our journeys.

This book is dedicated to my parents, Charles and Joan Mayberry. They laid the groundwork for my Christian faith and life. The core values that I hold dear to me today, I learned from them. The more I reflect upon their lives, I realize the most important things they held dear to their hearts. These values were passed down from their parents.

* Attending church regularly as a family
* Closeness of family
* There were rules in the family to follow, and that was how they showed their love
* Serving family and others
* Integrity
* A strong work ethic
* A strong faith in Jesus Christ, our Lord and Savior

I love and miss you, mom and dad!

Contents

Dedication   v

1. Building a Relationship with God — 3
2. Where is God? — 13
3. How do you see your life? — 29
4. God at work in your life — 35
5. Fruit of the Spirit – Inward Traits — 45
6. Fruit of the Spirit - Outward Traits — 57
7. The struggle is real — 67
8. Can you hear me now? — 73
9. Confiding in a friend — 79
10. Not Just on Sunday — 83
11. 9 Habits to put God in the Center of Your Life — 89
12. How do You Know it is Working? — 99
13. Where do we go from here? — 115

Introduction

In a world filled with constant distractions and the hustle and bustle of everyday life, we find ourselves longing for something more. As we navigate the challenges and complexities of our existence, we begin to realize that a void within our souls must be filled. With a heart full of curiosity and a desire for spiritual growth, we embark on a journey toward establishing or deepening our relationship with God. Armed with determination and an open mind, we seek guidance from wise mentors, explore various religious traditions, and immerse ourselves in the teachings of ancient scriptures.

You open yourself up to deeper insights and understanding by taking moments to pause and reflect. These moments of introspection and contemplation can lead to personal growth and transformation. Embrace these quiet moments as opportunities for self-discovery and positive change. We discover that connecting with God is not just about following rituals or adhering to predetermined doctrines. It is about embracing love, compassion, and gratitude as the foundation of this divine relationship.

We encounter others who share their experiences and insights along the way. Together, we form a supportive community that holds space for growth and transformation. We engage in meaningful discussions, share stories of personal breakthroughs, and inspire one another to keep moving forward on their spiritual path. As we delve deeper into our exploration, we uncover profound truths about ourselves and our purpose in life. We realize this journey is not just about finding God but also about finding ourselves – understanding our own values, passions, strengths, and weaknesses.

With each step forward, we experience moments of awe and wonder – moments when we feel the presence of something greater than ourselves guiding us toward divine connection. We witness miracles unfolding in unexpected ways – synchronicities that affirm our faith and validate their pursuit. This book serves as a roadmap for anyone seeking to establish a relationship with God or enhance an existing one. Embrace the power of mindfulness and gratitude to silence your mind and connect with something greater. Through prayer, acts of kindness, and nurturing gratitude, you can bring these practices into your daily life and unlock the profound presence of God. Let these practical tools guide you toward a more fulfilling and enlightened existence.

By using introspection, sharing relatable stories, and offering uplifting quotations, this book reminds all readers that the path to a profound connection with God is deeply personal. Embrace your own unique journey and let it inspire you on your spiritual journey. There is no right or wrong way to embark on this path – only the commitment to open your heart, surrender your doubts and fears, and trust in the divine unfolding of your own unique relationship.

As you turn the pages of this book, you will be inspired to look within, embrace your spirituality, and embark on a transformative journey toward a profound connection with God. It reminds you that no matter where you are on your path, you can always take steps toward deepening your relationship and experiencing the boundless love and guidance that awaits.

I

Building a Relationship with God

If you desire a relationship with God, you have taken the first step. This desire will keep you focused on growing that relationship. God wants a relationship with you but will not force Himself on you. Instead, He will patiently wait for you to start the connection. You will likely not just wake up one day and feel like you have become friends with God. It usually does not happen that way. Like in human relationships, building up a relationship takes time.

We have all sorts of relationships with others. Some of those would be family, acquaintances, colleagues at work, classmates, and lifelong friends. Not everyone we meet is going to want to hang out with you. Not everyone we hang out with is going to become a closer friend. That does not mean that we do not try to start friendships. Think about your closest relationships outside of your family. How did they become your closest friends? It usually starts with getting to know the other person. You start to spend more time with them.

You need time to get to know them, have fun together, and become more comfortable with each other. There are many ways to get to know each other and bond in a group setting. That's a lot better than nothing, but the real opportunities to connect often come up when it's just you and the other person talking.

Let's start from the beginning. You introduce yourself (or someone introduces you) to them and then start to get to know them. In the case of God, He already knows everything about you, but what do you know about Him? How were you introduced to Him, and what have you learned about Him through the Bible, church, or conversations with other Christians? Think back to your best friend and how you met. Initially, your conversations are light and upbeat. You do not dig into each other's personal life or get confrontational. We tend to do the same thing with our relationship with God. We get to know Him slowly and tend to try to keep our personal lives somewhat vague to Him, even though He already knows all about us. We learn from His teachings but do not initially apply everything we learn to our lives.

Next, you will lay down the foundation of the friendship. You will have more conversations and get to know each other more deeply. Sometimes this is planned with the goal of learning more about the other person, and sometimes it just happens through a normal conversation. It may be getting together over a cup of coffee or starting by being introduced to someone at a social gathering, and you realize you have some of the same interests or hobbies. That starts the conversation, and it grows from there. You do this with your relationship with God by attending church, studying your Bible, and being willing to show your quirky habits or flaws. Even though God already knows all this about you, we tend not to think about Him watching us.

Another factor that bonds people is when one helps the other. They can look back over the relationship and be able to think,

"We're pretty close. We've helped each other through some real rough times." Friends rely on each other for support through the hard times. So, you must know God will be there if you ever need Him. You can always count on Him to be there for you. He gives you strength, comfort, and healing. Friends are there for one another. That is what friends do.

People see their relationships as deeper and more rewarding when they can talk to each other about more weighty or personal topics, things they can't bring up with just anyone. It also feels good to know you've shown someone pieces of your real self, and they accept you for it. I think about Facebook and all the "friendships" you have. Most of what you learn about someone is the good side of their lives. Sure, they share when times are tough and want sympathy or support, but do they ever post the bad stuff they have done? Do they post about the things they are ashamed of? No relationship can withstand being built on secrets and lies, so it is essential to be open and honest. Not only do you need to be honest with God, but you also need to be honest with yourself.

To develop into a solid close relationship, it takes work. No matter how much you and your friends have in common, arguments and disagreements will arise at some point. Work through these bumps in the road with your friends. The same things apply to your relationship with God. Do you understand His point of view? When things do not go your way, do you blame it on God or work it out with Him and realize that it is all part of His will? I am not saying you should be quiet and not share your feelings with God. Open up to Him and express your feelings. That is one of the first steps toward resolving your differences. He will listen to everything you say and understand where you are coming from. Now it is your turn. You need to listen to God and understand where He is coming from. Your relationship will grow stronger as you have these honest conversations.

Let us go back to the beginning and what it takes to start a relationship with God. There are people you know but do not have a relationship with. You may know of God, but that does not mean you have a relationship with Him. In John 4:16, Jesus says, ...I am the way, the truth, and the light. No one comes to the Father except through me. So, the first step in beginning a relationship with God is choosing to walk with His Son. That requires three things of us:

Admission. It is important for us to acknowledge our imperfections and recognize that we all sin. By humbly recognizing our need for a Savior, we can find the guidance and redemption we require to lead better lives.

"for all have sinned and fall short of the glory of God," Romans 3:23 NIV

Note that it says **all** have sinned. How often do we think of the flaws and sins of others and ignore our own? We all need our Savior, Jesus Christ. We require that forgiveness to be able to get closer to God.

Belief. Believe that Jesus is the perfect Son of God who died on the cross (and rose again) to pay the penalty for our sins. That is powerful! He was perfect, and we are the ones sinning, yet He paid the ultimate price (His life) for us.

For God so loved the world that he gave his one and only Son, that whoever believes in him shall not perish but have eternal life. John 3:16 NIV

Confess Jesus as our Lord. Declare with conviction that Jesus is our Lord and Savior. Embrace the truth of His divinity and the salvation He brings to humanity. By professing this belief, we open ourselves up to a life of faith, hope, and redemption in His unfailing love.

If you declare with your mouth, "Jesus is Lord," and believe in your heart that God raised him from the dead, you will be saved. For it is with

your heart that you believe and are justified, and it is with your mouth that you profess your faith and are saved. Romans 10:9-10 NIV

Once we get through the first step in the relationship, we need to increase our efforts to build the relationship to a higher level. We must pray, study the Bible, and grow with others. Your interaction with other Christians, through the church, etc., helps to boost your relationship with God. This, in turn, will lead us to follow His commandments, serve others, and share the Gospel. His commandments can be found in Deuteronomy 5:6-21 (NIV).

6 "I am the Lord your God, who brought you out of Egypt, out of the land of slavery.

7 "You shall have no other gods before me.

8 "You shall not make for yourself an image in the form of anything in heaven above or on the earth beneath or in the waters below. 9 You shall not bow down to them or worship them; for I, the Lord your God, am a jealous God, punishing the children for the sin of the parents to the third and fourth generation of those who hate me, 10 but showing love to a thousand generations of those who love me and keep my commandments.

11 "You shall not misuse the name of the Lord your God, for the Lord will not hold anyone guiltless who misuses his name.

12 "Observe the Sabbath day by keeping it holy, as the Lord your God has commanded you. 13 Six days you shall labor and do all your work, 14 but the seventh day is a sabbath to the Lord your God. On it you shall not do any work, neither you, nor your son or daughter, nor your male or female servant, nor your ox, your donkey or any of your animals, nor any foreigner residing in your towns, so that your male and female servants may rest, as you do. 15 Remember that you were slaves in Egypt and that the Lord your God brought you out of there with a mighty hand and an outstretched arm. Therefore the Lord your God has commanded you to observe the Sabbath day.

16 "Honor your father and your mother, as the Lord your God has

commanded you, so that you may live long and that it may go well with you in the land the Lord your God is giving you.

17 "You shall not murder.

18 "You shall not commit adultery.

19 "You shall not steal.

20 "You shall not give false testimony against your neighbor.

21 "You shall not covet your neighbor's wife. You shall not set your desire on your neighbor's house or land, his male or female servant, his ox or donkey, or anything that belongs to your neighbor."

Besides following His commandments, we will serve others and share the Gospel. Doing all these things brings us closer to God and strengthens our relationship. He will become your closest friend, and all the traits of a close friend will be there.

"Good things as well as bad, you know, are caught by a kind of infection. If you want to get warm, you must stand near the fire: if you want to be wet, you must get into the water. If you want joy, power, peace, eternal life, you must get close to, or even into, the thing that has them. They are not a sort of prize which God could, if He chose, just hand out to anyone. They are a great fountain of energy and beauty spurting up at the very centre of reality. If you are close to it, the spray will wet you: if you are not, you will remain dry." ~ C. S. Lewis

If you truly want to strengthen your bond with God, it's essential to seek out the places where His presence is strongest. Open your heart and mind, and you'll find yourself in sacred spaces that nourish your spiritual connection. It's like seeking out those places and experiences that bring you closer to God and make you feel His divine presence. Whether it's through prayer, meditation, attending religious gatherings, or simply spending time in nature, finding your own unique way to connect with God is all about creating a personal and meaningful relationship.

Humans are defined by their relationships more than any other part of their lives. Relationships tell people about our past, our present, and our future. Our core values serve as the guiding light that shapes our interactions and connections with others. In the vast expanse of the real world, the company we choose to keep speaks volumes about our character and the principles we hold dear. It is through these relationships that our true essence is revealed, showcasing not only our individuality but also how we align with those who share similar values. Each connection we cultivate becomes a testament to who we are and a reflection of the positive impact we strive to make in this world. Embrace meaningful connections, for they have the power to shape us into better versions of ourselves and create a ripple effect that spreads inspiration far beyond our immediate circle. To that point, the only relationship that defines who we genuinely are is our relationship with God.

We can see that humanity is unique just by looking back to the Garden of Eden. Genesis teaches us that we are the only creature made "in God's image." We are the only thing in this world with an inherent value, the only creation Jesus died for, and the only creation God wants a relationship with. This cannot be taken away from us. We have seen over time where certain people have been denied rights, but in this case, we cannot be denied a relationship with God. He believes in us; we are unique. Though, a relationship with God must be on His terms. Our relationship with God defines how we see others. We should see others as God sees them. The people we meet in all situations are also made in God's image.

Look back at how you found God and started the path toward a relationship with Him. It may have been while sitting in a church pew or conversing with a coworker over coffee. A church or our peers may help us to have a relationship with God. They may give us direction and show us how to listen to Him and act according to His guidance. Ultimately, the relationship you will develop will be a personal one. It may have similar traits to someone else's relationship, but it will not be the same. I have attended many churches, and many feel you should believe precisely like they do and try to put your relationship in a box. I do not think God wants this in His relationship with you. I feel He wants to get to know you very personally and for you to know Him the same way. Unlike your relationship with a church, a relationship with God comes from His amazing love and grace reaching out to us. Since creation, it's always been His desire to reveal Himself to us. In the beginning, God desired an everlasting, loving relationship with man. Unfortunately, Adam and Eve chose to reject God's commands and produced sin, separating man from God. Sin brought the breakdown of a relationship with God, resulting in shame and judgment.

Religion cannot restore this relationship with God. No human ritual, deed, or sacrifice can provide payment or absolution for our sins. It is God's will to save us and establish an everlasting relationship with Him. Jesus Christ's voluntary death on the cross delivered the power to redeem us. A personal relationship with God begins with knowing His Son, Jesus Christ.

How is your relationship with God? Is Christ the center of your life? We must start with the fundamentals to fully understand our relationship with God and where we want it to go. Do you believe in God? This is a simple question; you probably answered yes if you are reading this book. But what I am asking is if you genuinely believe in God. That is where it gets more complicated. It seems simple enough to believe in God, but why would we ever have stress if we had a strong belief? Why would we ever doubt His will for us? Having a relationship with God means being able not to doubt or deny any of His work and being able to submit to His will. Truly embracing a life of purpose and meaning means aligning our intentions with the divine presence of God. It involves surrendering our own personal agendas and making room for God's plans to unfold in our lives. By prioritizing God's interests and the well-being of His family, we create a harmonious balance that enriches not only our own lives but also the lives of those around us. To fully embrace this journey, we must be open to receiving God's critique with humility and grace. Understanding that His guidance is rooted in love and wisdom, we willingly submit ourselves to His direction. By doing so, we allow Him to shape us into the best versions of ourselves. Remember, walking this path may not always be easy. There may be challenges along the way, but it is through these trials that we grow stronger in faith and resilience. Trusting in God's plan for us allows us to navigate life's twists and turns with an unwavering sense of peace.

At the very least, you must do nothing that goes against your conscience and not do anything shameful. That which rebels against or resists God you absolutely must not do, and you must not do anything that disturbs the work or life of the church. Be just and honorable in everything you do and ensure your every action is presentable before God. Although the flesh may sometimes be weak, you must be able to put the interests of God's family first, without greed for personal profit, without doing anything selfish or despicable, often reflecting on yourself. In this way, you will be able to often live before God, and you will have a close relationship with God.

At a minimum, are your intentions aligned with His teachings? Look at your choices and determine if they are self-driven or for fulfilling God's glory. There may be parts of you that are weak or disobedient, but if your views and your intentions are correct, and if your relationship with God is good, then you are qualified to be made perfect by God. If you do not have the right relationship with God and act for the sake of the flesh or your family, regardless of how hard you work, it will be for nothing. No matter what you are doing, consider the following when you are doing it: What will God think if I do this? Will it benefit my brothers and sisters? Will it be beneficial to the work in God's house? Whether in prayer, fellowship, speech, work, or contact with others, examine your intentions and how they reflect on your relationship with God.

God takes the initiative in the relationship, but we must be active participants. He is constantly communicating with us through His word and history. He comes to us in Jesus Christ, His teachings, in the apostles, through His word, and speaks to us. We "feel" this communication through the presence of the Holy Spirit, who dwells within us. The path is our lives moving towards God while He is coming towards us. So let the Bible be where God meets you and speaks to you, and let the Bible be where you speak back to him. The relationship is in this communion: Him to us and us to Him.

Those who have a personal relationship with God include God in their daily lives. They pray to Him, read His word, and meditate on verses to get to know Him better. Those with a personal relationship with God pray for wisdom, the best asset we could ever have. They take their requests to Him, asking in Jesus' name. Jesus is the one who loves us enough to give His life for us, and He is the one who bridged the gap between us and God.

This personal relationship with God is not as hard to find as we might think. As soon as we become children of God, we receive the Holy Spirit, who will begin to work on our hearts. We should pray without ceasing, read the Bible, and join a Bible-believing church; all these things will help us to grow spiritually. Trusting in God to get us through each day and believing that He is our sustainer is the way to have a relationship with Him. Although we may not see changes immediately, we will begin to see them over time, and all the truths will become clear.

An intimate relationship with God is available to every believer, but it must be cultivated, nurtured, and developed like any other relationship.

2

Where is God?

If you want a relationship with God, you must go where God is. But where is God, and how do I find Him? To experience a profound and meaningful connection with God, you must seek His presence on a heartfelt quest. Open your heart and let it guide you toward a fulfilling relationship with the ultimate source of love and wisdom. The question arises: where does one find God? The answer lies not in your physical location but rather within the depths of your own being. It is through this inner journey that you will discover an unbreakable bond with something greater than yourself – an eternal source of love and wisdom. In these simple moments, you will realize that God is omnipresent – in every blade of grass, every twinkling star, and every beating heart. Furthermore, finding God requires unwavering faith combined with sincere devotion. Engage in spiritual practices that resonate with your soul – whether it be prayer, meditation, or acts of kindness towards others. These acts serve as pathways to connect with the divine energy that permeates all existence.

Let's start with "Who is God?"

> or through him, God created everything in the heavenly realms and on earth. He made the things we can see and the things we can't see—such as thrones, kingdoms, rulers, and authorities in the unseen world. Everything was created through him and for him.
> Colossians 1:16 (NLT)

God is our Creator. He created the entire universe and everything and everyone in it. He is omnipresent, meaning He is always in all places; as Job 34:21 (NLT) states, *"For God watches how people live; he sees everything they do.* It is reinforced in Psalms 139:7 (NLT) *I can never escape from your Spirit! I can never get away from your presence!* He is omnipotent, all-powerful. In Matthew 19:26 it says, *"But Jesus looked at them and said, "With man this is impossible, but with God all things are possible."* Read that again. With God, all things are possible. Not some, but **all**. That is a powerful statement about a mighty God.

Sometimes the Bible also speaks about where God is in more specific terms. For example, He is often mentioned as dwelling in heaven. In addition, God has revealed Himself visibly in a variety of ways. These include God's appearance to Moses in the burning bush (Exodus 3) and His presence with the Israelites in the wilderness.

In the New Testament, Jesus comes to earth as the second Person of the Triune God to reveal God to humanity. John 1:1 defines Jesus as the "Word" and calls Him God. John 1:14 reads, *So the Word became human and made his home among us. He was full of unfailing love and faithfulness. And we have seen his glory, the glory of the Father's one and only Son.* He lived, died, rose again, and ascended to the Father in heaven.

After this, God sent the Holy Spirit to live within those who believe in Him. So, Ephesians 1:13 teaches, *"And now you Gentiles have also heard the truth, the Good News that God saves you. And when you believed in Christ, he identified you as his own by giving you the Holy Spirit, whom he promised long ago."*

In summary, though God is omnipresent, He can also be present in other ways precisely. Many of these ways were revealed in the Old Testament. Jesus Christ came as God with us. The Holy Spirit now dwells within those who believe in Jesus as Lord.

But if God is always present and all-powerful, where is God when it hurts, and life is difficult? This is a question people ponder all the time. How can I be hurt so badly if I have a close relationship with God? Jesus faced this challenge on the cross when He asked, "My God, my God, why have you forsaken me?" (Matthew 27:46). In His time of pain, where was God the Father? Did He not care, or was He not there? Christ's pain on the cross later served as part of God's glorious plan to reveal the resurrected Jesus and bring salvation to many. God the Father knew these things had to take place for His ultimate will, the salvation of all, to take place.

This insight also applies to when we go through times of struggle in our own lives. We tend to rely upon emotions. These emotions question whether God is there because He does not appear to be at work during our struggle. Yet just as with Jesus on the cross, God is still at work even when it does not feel like it.

> *And we know that God causes everything to work together for the good of those who love God and are called according to his purpose for them.* Romans 8:28 (NLT)

He uses **everything** to work together for good. He does not just use the good things to make good things happen. We must trust that

He is with us, loves us, and has a purpose for our lives. When we are struggling through the hardships of life, we can rest in the fact that His power is made perfect in weakness. We should celebrate these hardships and difficulties.

> But he said to me, "My grace is sufficient for you, for my power is made perfect in weakness." Therefore, I will boast all the more gladly about my weaknesses, so that Christ's power may rest on me. That is why, for Christ's sake, I delight in weaknesses, in insults, in hardships, in persecutions, in difficulties. For when I am weak, then I am strong. 2 Corinthians 12:9-10 (NIV)

Are you longing for a close relationship with God? Do others have that relationship that you desire? Are we waiting for Him to come to us, or are we out there seeking a relationship with Him? God is not going to turn away a relationship. He is always there, patiently waiting for us to come closer to Him.

It is undeniable that some Christians seem to experience a much closer intimacy with God than others. They appear to enjoy a reverent familiarity with Him that is foreign to us. Is it a matter of favoritism on the part of God? Or do such people qualify in some way for that desirable intimacy? Are there secrets we may discover that would admit us to a similar intimacy?

A familiar story in the Bible is used in many churches as the basis for developing a closer relationship with God.

THE ROAD TO EMMAUS

> That same day two of Jesus' followers were walking to the village of Emmaus, seven miles[a] from Jerusalem. As they walked along, they were

talking about everything that had happened. As they talked and discussed these things, Jesus himself suddenly came and began walking with them. But God kept them from recognizing him.

He asked them, "What are you discussing so intently as you walk along?"

They stopped short, sadness written across their faces. Then one of them, Cleopas, replied, "You must be the only person in Jerusalem who hasn't heard about all the things that have happened there the last few days." "What things?" Jesus asked.

"The things that happened to Jesus, the man from Nazareth," they said. "He was a prophet who did powerful miracles, and he was a mighty teacher in the eyes of God and all the people. But our leading priests and other religious leaders handed him over to be condemned to death, and they crucified him. We had hoped he was the Messiah who had come to rescue Israel. This all happened three days ago.

"Then some women from our group of his followers were at his tomb early this morning, and they came back with an amazing report. They said his body was missing, and they had seen angels who told them Jesus is alive! Some of our men ran out to see, and sure enough, his body was gone, just as the women had said."

Then Jesus said to them, "You foolish people! You find it so hard to believe all that the prophets wrote in the Scriptures. Wasn't it clearly predicted that the Messiah would have to suffer all these things before entering his glory?" Then Jesus took them through the writings of Moses and all the prophets, explaining from all the Scriptures the things concerning himself.

By this time, they were nearing Emmaus and the end of their journey. Jesus acted as if he were going on, but they begged him, "Stay the night with us, since it is getting late." So he went home with them. As they sat down to eat, he took the bread and blessed it. Then he broke it and gave it to them. Suddenly, their eyes were opened, and they recognized him. And at that moment he disappeared!

They said to each other, "Didn't our hearts burn within us as he talked with us on the road and explained the Scriptures to us?" And within the hour they were on their way back to Jerusalem. There they found the eleven disciples and the others who had gathered with them, who said, "The Lord has really risen! He appeared to Peter."

Then the two from Emmaus told their story of how Jesus had appeared to them as they were walking along the road, and how they had recognized him as he was breaking the bread.

Luke 24:13-35 (NLT)

They were worried since they had heard about the angel's announcement that Jesus was alive, but still had doubts about the resurrection. So immersed were they in their sadness that they could not recognize Jesus in the person walking alongside them. Are we going through life and being wrapped up in our everyday lives that we do not see Jesus among us? That does not mean He is not there, but we do not see him.

The two disciples had a long walk ahead of them that day. And leaving Jerusalem was like leaving behind their faith in Jesus. But Jesus comes to meet them to transform their hearts. Jesus helps them to talk about their worries to dissipate them. Jesus joining them as they go along their way was as incredible to them as it is when He joins us along our way! When you come down to our level, follow us and seek us in the hustle and bustle of each day. Lord, grant us a childlike spirit, pure eyes, and a clear head so we may recognize you when you come without any outward sign of your glory.

Some people approach their interaction with God as an athlete on a playing field. God is in the stands, cheering them on. He is a spectator. They look up to Him for accolades for doing things right. He joins the rest of the spectators in voicing disapproval when they do something wrong. That is not the case. He is on the playing field with us. He is a coach, physical conditioning trainer, doctor, and sports psychologist, to name a few. Why are some people unable to recognize His presence?

As you go through this book, I want you to be able to open your eyes to see Him. Enable yourself to hear what He has to say. Feel His presence in your life and His spirit in your body. Our body is the physical realm in this material world. We have the five senses to help us in this experience—sight, hearing, taste, smell, and touch. But God is not of this world. The disciples and the people that lived when Jesus lived on Earth had the opportunity to experience God with these senses. Still, there were non-believers. We are always asking for a sign. We seek a sign from God proving His presence or will. This will not be enough because they are all around us, and we must know them.

Our soul is the psychological realm of intangible items like thoughts, feelings, and decision-making capabilities. How do we tap into our soul? How do we use these traits to see and experience God? For example, we experience sadness and joy—the pain of our heartbreak or the excitement of our accomplishments. We can use these feelings to experience God's presence. We can use them to bring us closer to God.

We sometimes associate our soul with being our spirit. 2 Timothy 4:28 says The Lord be with your spirit.

> *Then the Lord God formed a man from the dust of the ground and breathed into his nostrils the breath of life, and the man became a living being.* Genesis 2:7

The breath of life is the spirit that God planted within us. Our human spirit is the deepest part of our being. It is through our spirit that we can communicate with God. Picture your car radio from when they used to have dial tuners, unlike the digital ones in current days. You turn it to a frequency, and through the airwaves, the signal comes from the radio station, is deciphered by the radio, and plays your favorite songs. Do you see the airwaves? No. You could only hear the radio station broadcast with the radio as the receiver. That is how your spirit works with God. Your spirit interprets the communication from God and lets you "hear" Him.

Our spirit was created by God so that we can communicate with Him. Our body and soul have specific functions; only our hearts can contact God. We can see this from numerous verses, including John 4:24: "God is Spirit, and those who worship Him must worship in spirit and truthfulness." To contact (or worship) God, who is Spirit, we must use our spirit.

Like how God initially breathed our human spirits into us, Jesus breathed the gift of the Holy Spirit into the disciples in John 20:22. *And with that he breathed on them and said, "Receive the Holy Spirit.* So, as we accept Jesus Christ as our Savior, we receive the Holy Spirit. It is like that secret decoder ring. We can now experience all that God has to offer. We now have that translator. We have the means to have two-way conversations with God.

As with learning a new sport or hobby, we must practice our skills. The best way to exercise our spirit is through prayer. The more we use this communication tool to interact with God, the better it will work. As in any relationship, we should have open communication. Do you have specific times to call friends or speak to your spouse? Probably not. You communicate when it feels right. Sometimes, it is in person; other times, it may require a phone call. We used to communicate through letters sent through the mail. That is almost a lost art since the internet was invented, and we now have access to email. If you are in a rush and do not have much to say, it may be done by sending a text message to the other person. The same principle can be applied to prayer. It does not have to be at a specific time each day, in a particular place. It can be long or short. The main thing is to communicate often.

To pray means to communicate with God. That can mean thanking Him, praising Him, confessing something you've done wrong, or expressing a need you have. It can even mean just talking to Him like a friend. People often say prayer is just talking to God as you would to anyone else. A relationship with God is indeed like our other relationships. But there is at least one unique factor: we can't rely on the senses of sight, sound, or touch to connect with God.

Perhaps the best place to begin is by clarifying that prayer is more about talking **with** God than just talking **to** Him. What you believe about God and your relationship with Him is fundamental to how you will learn to speak with Him. People pray for all sorts of reasons. Some pray to get comfort and strength in troubling times. It can be a solace, allowing individuals to find peace within themselves as they share their concerns, fears, or worries with God. Remember that prayer is not limited to burdensome moments alone —it can also be an expression of gratitude for blessings received or simply an opportunity to cultivate a sense of mindfulness and reflection in daily life. Each person's reasons for praying may differ based on their unique experiences, beliefs, and spiritual journey.

> "We were promised suffering. They were part of the program. We were even told, 'Blessed are they that mourn,' and I accept it. I've got nothing that I hadn't bargained for. Of course, it is different when the thing happens to oneself, not others, and in reality, not imagination." C.S. Lewis

Many people's lives are full of suffering. How do we make sense of this suffering? Why does God allow suffering? Why does he allow the innocent and righteous to suffer? Where is God when I'm hurting? An older man groans in pain, longing for release. A young woman loses her husband in a motorcycle accident, leaving her to raise her three children alone. We cringe at the horror of Auschwitz. We're confronted and offended by such misery. We often search for hidden meaning within suffering itself or seek explanations from other places.

Where is God when we are suffering?

In 2020, we learned a lot about suffering. A global pandemic was worsening, and relatives and friends died. Others were deathly ill. Everyone reacts to suffering in different ways. You may think you know how someone else feels through their situation, but it may affect them differently. The extent of suffering in the world raises profound questions about the nature of God and his involvement in human life. Why do innocent people suffer if God is all good, all-powerful, and all-loving? Where was God through this? Why did He let this happen? What good could come from this?

Some people draw closer to God through their suffering. They go to church more and try reconnecting with their faith. During the pandemic, this was not an option. The question of where God is during our suffering has been around for a long time. He experienced our woes by becoming a man (Jesus) and dying on the cross. So, He knows our pain and suffering intimately. One passage that can give you comfort in suffering is Isaiah.

When you pass through the waters I will be with you; and through the rivers, they shall not overwhelm you; when you walk through fire you shall not be burned, and the flame shall not consume you. Isaiah 43:2 (NLT)

In this verse, God tells the Jewish people that He will be with them in their most troubling times, supporting them through them, giving them the strength to move beyond them, and delivering them out of danger without harm. The waters they passed through reference the parting of the Red Sea when God opened it for miles to allow the Israelites to walk on dry land through the sea (Exodus 14:21-22). Then God let the walls of the sea close and destroy Israel's enemies. God suddenly dried up the Jordan river as a band of priests carrying the ark of the covenant stood at the river's edge. (Joshua 3:14-17). This happened when Jordan typically would have been overflowing its banks. The ark represented the presence of God. The fire represented when God protected Shadrach, Meshach, and Abednego when Nebuchadnezzar had his soldiers throw them in a furnace. Still, instead of killing these three, it killed the soldiers standing by the furnace (Daniel 3). The tragedy and suffering were not prevented; God helped them get through them. He gives us this same reassurance. One thing we know about grief is how we depend on others to help us get through it. God wants us to rely entirely on Him to get us through it. It brings Him glory when we admit our weakness and that God is holding us together. As fellow believers, we can show God's love by comforting each other in our own profound and unique ways.

But notice God's purpose for his comfort. As we look to God for comfort and hope in suffering, he means to spur us on to comfort others afflicted with the same comfort we've received from God.

God comforts us so that we can comfort others. God grants us mercy so that we can be merciful to others. God stands wholeheartedly with us in our suffering so that we will stand wholeheartedly with others suffering. God never leaves us alone in our suffering so that we won't leave others alone in theirs.

Where is God when we are lonely?

Loneliness is what we feel when we're isolated from others. It does not necessarily mean we are physically separated, but more about feeling disconnected or alienated from them. It may be where we think they do not understand us.

We are not designed to be lonely but connected to others and God. God did not place Adam alone in the Garden of Eden. Yet, He allows us to be lonely, so we yearn for companionship. We need to use this loneliness to guide us back to the one who can fill that need to be understood and fully loved.

Even when you feel alone, God is still with you. But if He is so near to you, why do you not feel His presence or have His peace? Just because you do not feel His presence does not mean He has left your side. He will never leave you. It comes down to that crazy human mind we have. We "feel" we are alone. So, how do we overcome this feeling?

Loneliness can serve a greater purpose in our lives - to help us draw closer to God. In the midst of our busy schedules, we often struggle to make time for spiritual connection. However, when we are alone, God can speak to us directly and have our undivided attention. I understand that loneliness can be a challenging emotion to experience. Loneliness can offer an opportunity for introspection, self-discovery, and a deeper connection with God. It allows us to tune into our inner thoughts and feelings, making us more receptive to God's presence and messages.

Sometimes, reaching out for companionship or engaging in community service can help alleviate feelings of isolation while strengthening connections with God and others. Ultimately, it is important to remember that each person's spiritual journey is unique. Whatever path you choose, know that you are not alone in seeking spiritual fulfillment — countless individuals are navigating similar experiences along the way.

Where is God in our shortcomings?

When I am weak, he is strong. Paul firmly believed this and wrote in a letter to Corinth. *But he said to me, "My grace is sufficient for you, for my power is made perfect in weakness." Therefore I will boast all the more gladly about my weaknesses, so that Christ's power may rest on me.* 2 Corinthians 12:9

Paul has reversed boasting and gloating. It is not so much that he could not care less that others may think he is feeble. It is that he was weak, and he needed everybody to know it. The strength of God is made perfect in our shortcomings. When we are feeble, we have power in the grace of Jesus. When we feel powerless, we are to go to Christ and receive strength from him. When we see ourselves as being decisive in our capabilities or assets, we are enticed to manage God's job alone, which allows pride to set in. However, when we are deficient and weak, and we allow God to use us by instilling within us his power, then, at that point, we are more powerful than we would be if we were on our own.

With your relationship with God comes benefits you may not have sought. With His lead, you can become His best version of yourself. How often do couples start dating, and then some of their shortcomings appear? Then, it moves into a pattern of changing or trying to change your partner's behavior, dress, lifestyle, etc. How does it make you feel? Are you stubborn about changing? You may not see anything wrong with your current self. But, when we allow God to change our lives, we can become much more than we are currently.

The Holy Spirit can guide you to your better self. But our human nature does not allow us to be shown because we want to be in charge. In my Sunday school class, a member told us what his friend had told him about his spiritual growth. He said he was always driving, and Jesus was the passenger for most of his life. Finally, one day, he realized he needed to let God drive. Do you need to let God drive?

Where is God in our relationships?

God is often seen as a source of guidance and comfort in our relationships. We look to Him for advice when facing difficult decisions, for strength when we are feeling weak, and for hope when we feel lost. Whether it is in our romantic relationships or with friends and family, God can be a powerful presence that helps us navigate the complexities of life. He can provide us with the wisdom to make wise choices and the courage to stand up for what is right. Ultimately, His presence in our relationships can help us develop meaningful connections with those around us.

It is often said that we should find God in our relationships. But where should we look for Him? Is He in the good times or the bad? Or maybe He is in both. So, let's explore where we might find God in our relationships. Perhaps the answer lies in learning to see Him in all aspects of our lives. After all, relationships are a big part of living our lives to the fullest.

When we think about where to find God in our relationships, it's important to remember that He is present in all aspects of our lives. He is there when we're happy and when we're struggling, when we're at our best and when we're at our worst. We can find Him in the people we love and the strangers we meet. We have heard over the years that our goal should be for others to see God through us and our actions. But let's turn the table and look for God in others. Think of your close relationships with friends, co-workers, or family. Can you see God in their actions?

There are certain places where we can look for God in our relationships. He can be found in the highs and lows, in the good and bad times. He is present in laughter, tears, and give and take.

We can find Him when reaching out to others and being vulnerable. He is there in the simple act of being present with someone else. But are we aware of Him? He is always present. So where should we look for God in our relationships? Everywhere.

Where is God in our complicated relationships?

Our relationships can be complicated and confusing at times, leaving us with the question of where God fits into the equation. It is easy to feel like God has stepped away from our lives when we face difficult times or struggles, but the truth is that He is always right there with us, present in our relationships and in every situation. He never leaves us alone in the dark, even if we cannot see or feel Him there. Whether it's a relationship between two people or between a person and their faith, God can be found in all aspects of our lives. He can provide comfort, guidance, and strength when needed.

If you are struggling to see God in your most difficult relationships, here are five ways that may help you:

1. Pray for the person you are struggling with.
2. Ask God to help you see the situation from His perspective.
3. Seek wise counsel from a trusted friend or pastor.
4. Read scripture passages that speak to your situation.
5. Look for ways that God is working despite the difficulty.

It is often in our most difficult relationships that we can find God. We all have difficult relationships in our lives, whether it be with a family member, co-worker, or even ourselves. In these times of struggles and strife, it can be hard to see where God is in the midst of it all. But we must remember that He is always with us and He is there to provide us with grace and peace during these trying times. Prayer can also be a powerful tool to help us find solace in difficult relationships. By praying for guidance and grace, we can find the strength to persevere through any situation. By trying to see the other person's perspective, praying for them, and showing them grace, we can begin to see God working in our lives.

3

How do you see your life?

Do you need a new pair of glasses? How well do you see? When you look in the mirror, what do you see? I am not talking about the bedhead hair first thing in the morning, the face without makeup, or after your grooming. Instead, I am talking about your inner being. What is going on inside of you? Are you anxious today? Are you joyful? What is your mood? Do you have a sense of purpose in your life? Are you going down the path that you anticipated? Are you living up to your potential?

That may take more than just staring at the mirror. I want you to see yourself and form an opinion, even if it is not as positive as you would like. I go to the eye doctor yearly to have my eyes tested, and my eyesight progressively worsens. I need new glasses to be able to see clearer. What if you need new glasses to see yourself clearer?

That may not be possible but try this. If you looked at yourself through God's eyes, what would He see? Is He going to like what He sees? I know God can see every flaw in me and every sin I commit. But what He also sees is my potential. He likes that. God sees our potential, sees who and what we are becoming. He considers the entire process going on in our lives. God sees the big picture. Others may see us as we are or make assumptions based on our past and origin. Take, for example, a job interview. The interviewer judges the job candidate based on their past. God, on the other hand, knows we can become more Christ-like with His help and guidance.

Sounds easy. Just look for God's direction and follow it. This is where the new pair of glasses comes in. We need to change how we look for God in our lives. He is always by our side, even when we do not recognize Him. We need to believe in our potential the way God does. The more we study His word in the Bible, the more we can see the direction we need to take and the steps to grow. Things sometimes go differently than we want them to.

> *"For my thoughts are not your thoughts, neither are your ways my ways, declares the Lord. For as the heavens are higher than the earth, so are my ways higher than your ways and my thoughts than your thoughts."* Isaiah 55:8-9 (NIV)

The idea that God has a plan suggests a higher purpose behind the events that unfold in our lives. While it can be difficult to comprehend why certain things happen, faith allows people to trust that there is greater wisdom at work. This belief encourages individuals to embrace change and look for personal growth and transformation opportunities. Accepting unforeseen circumstances as part of God's plan encourages people to seek understanding, strength, and guidance during times of uncertainty or difficulty. It can also inspire them to live intentionally, aligning their actions with what they believe to be God's will.

> *"And we know that in all things God works for the good of those who love him, who have been called according to his purpose"*
> Romans 8:28 (NIV)

The verse highlights God's purpose and will as the ultimate goal. It emphasizes that we are invited to participate in His plan. Additionally, it states that God works in all things to benefit those who love Him. However, it is important to note that this does not imply that everything will always be good but will ultimately work out for our own good. In difficult circumstances or challenging times, God orchestrates everything for our ultimate benefit. Emphasizing those who love Him and are called according to His purpose suggests an active role we can play in aligning ourselves with His will. Do you remember having to take some nasty medicine, but you did it because it was good for you? The main thing to think about is your potential in God's eyes. Are you going to believe in the same potential?

Think about the start of a new year. This is often an excellent time to hit the reset button. We tell ourselves that this year is going to be different. This year is going to be the best year ever. Making a "fresh start" isn't just a figure of speech; it's a psychological concept that has inspired much discussion over the years. Some people believe fresh starts can be an excellent way to motivate ourselves and improve our chances of reaching various goals while leaving unhealthy habits in the past. On the other hand, some argue that wiping the slate clean is only beneficial in certain circumstances.

A study by Hengchen Dai identifies the "fresh start effect" as a person's ability to disassociate past performance outcomes from their current or future goals. The fresh start effect is most potent around the new year. However, as mentioned, other meaningful occasions can spark a fresh start. For example, Hengchen states, "The popularity of New Year's resolutions suggests that people are more likely to tackle their goals immediately following salient temporal landmarks."

In other words, from a psychological perspective, we associate specific days (such as the 1st of January) with the symbolic act of metaphorically hitting life's reset button. At the end of the year, we see the start of a new calendar year as an opportunity to regain our focus, update our targets, and decide on new goals. It's no coincidence that gym memberships spike in January or that doctors get more patient calls about quitting smoking in the New Year. This is when we all want to make meaningful changes in our lives. Fast forward to the end of January, and how many of us are still dedicated to those new goals? Have you gotten complacent? What is stopping you from achieving those goals? For many, it is limits we put on ourselves. We start to have doubts about whether we can accomplish what we want to do. It is that self-doubt that gets in our way in many cases.

I attended a conference close to 15 years ago and participated in a session about how we are the main roadblock to our success. It is self-doubt that creeps into our thoughts and then sabotages our plans. The speaker asked volunteers to share one of their biggest goals and why they felt we needed to achieve them. I spoke up and said I always wanted to write a book on leadership. I was passionate about my thoughts on the subject but needed to improve my writing skills. I dreaded having to do an essay in school. I had started writing my potential book numerous times, but I would get down two pages of thoughts and then go blank.

The speaker told me I was the only one who felt I could not be a writer and needed to get out of my way. That resonated with me. A friend in the session turned to me and said, "I am anxious to read your book; now go write it." I was still "in my way" when I hit another wall when I sat down to write in the fall of 2010. That night, I turned to God and prayed about it. I asked Him if I was wasting my time trying to write a book. I had no material to put down on paper and wondered if I should give up on this dream. Finally, I dosed off to sleep, wondering what He thought about my ambitions that did not align with my previous skill sets or desires.

I woke up in the middle of the night with a thought on my mind. Faith-Based Leadership. These were just three words that had popped into my head. I did not know what they meant, but I felt they were important enough not to forget them. Many times, when you wake up from a dream, you can tell someone about the dream right away, but if you wait ten minutes, those thoughts are gone. I was worried this would be the case. So, I got up, wrote down those three words, and returned to bed. Little did I know then that this was God talking to me.

The following day, I thought about faith-based leadership and what that meant to me. I realized that I was so passionate about how to lead because it tied back to my religious beliefs. Those principles are what define my leadership style. So, I started writing again, and the words began to flow. That Christmas, I got a Kindle and started downloading about every free book I could find on writing and self-publishing. In September 2011, my first book, *Faith Guided Leadership*, was published. In 2012, I started the website faithguided-leadership.com and began blogging each week about how God was active in my life and how you can apply the same principles.

I tell this story often because it shows how our minds limit our potential. It highlights the limitations our minds impose on our potential. It emphasizes the importance of recognizing that God sees our true potential, and by allowing Him to guide us, we can unlock it. This prompts a thought-provoking question: Are you solely relying on your own efforts, or are you working in conjunction with God to achieve your fullest potential? By reflecting on this question, one can explore the power of surrendering control and embracing divine guidance in order to reach new heights in personal growth and achievement.

4

God at work in your life

Everyone has a story of how they came to know God and professed their faith to our Lord and Savior, Jesus Christ. I find reading about individuals written in the gospels meeting Jesus for the first time and their reactions interesting. When Mary first met Jesus, He cast seven demons out of her. She never took this for granted; this gratitude drew her closer to Him. She followed Jesus and learned as much as she could from Him. There was nothing special about her. She was just an everyday person. He picked her out to heal her. He brought her into His life and impacted her forever. Because of her faith and her example, her name has lived far past her earthly life.

We also learn that your past does not matter when you are with Christ. We can only assume that she was probably rejected in town since she had demons. She probably felt isolated and hopeless. Many around us feel the same way. But that did not stop Jesus from loving her and caring for her. She was set free that day from the things that tormented her inside. We all can be freed from what troubles us inside. It may be fears, anxiety, hopelessness, loneliness, rejection, etc.

When you reach out to Him, He will free you from your past. He will transform you into a new person by forgiving your sins. Of course, this happens instantly, but the relationship builds as we learn more about Him.

A perfect example of how instantaneous this transformation happens is the story of Jesus' crucifixion. This thief had reached a low point in his life. His checkered past caught up to him, and he was nailed to the cross and left to die. Yet, think about the level of faith he must have had. He saw Jesus dying on the cross next to him and people ridiculing Jesus as though He was not the Messiah since He could not save Himself. Yet, despite all of that, the thief still believed in Him. Because of this faith, the thief would have been the first to be in Heaven with Jesus. That is powerful when you think of the thief's past.

The thief was not influenced by peer pressure. If he had given in to peer pressure, he would have been mocking Jesus with the rest of them. But, because of his faith, Jesus saved him. He was forgiven of all his sins and gained salvation that day on the cross.

Take a moment to think back to your story. Did it begin as a child or as an adult? Were there significant moments in your life that "sealed the deal" even though you had already professed your faith years or decades ago? All our stories are unique. They may have similarities, but they are our own story. Do you compare your walk with Christ with what others are doing and experiencing?

Maybe you are reading this book and have not yet started your relationship with God. You may still be in the exploratory stage. I hope I have given you numerous reasons to bring Jesus into your life. Do not be ashamed of your past transgressions. He will set you free from them. Ask God to move within you and set you free. You do not need to do this at a church or in front of others. This is personal between you and God. Now may be an excellent time for those already in a relationship to renew their focus.

We are constantly comparing ourselves with others. It is human nature. Whether it be almost like a competition between who has more "stuff" or who is more popular, we compare ourselves to our peers and shouldn't. This passage of Scripture comes to mind. *Don't copy the customs and behaviors of this world, but let God transform you into a new person by changing the way you think. Then you will learn to know God's will for you, which is good, pleasing, and perfect.* (Romans 12:2) I have learned this firsthand in management throughout my career. Early on, I tended to "follow the crowd" and what was important to them was important to me. I had to "get ahead" and get that promotion at all costs. It cost me a lot. It cost me money due to several moves from city to city and state to state. It cost me relationships since I put my career above my spouse and family. It cost me my integrity since I was not leading people as I knew I should. I am glad I figured that out, albeit later in my career than I should have.

You could say I was born again. I renewed my relationship with Christ. I never felt I had lost the connection, but I had truly lost focus. I have had to use the reset button throughout my life. Yet, he has always welcomed me back with open arms. In Luke 15:11-32 (NIV), Jesus tells a parable about the prodigal son.

Jesus continued: "There was a man who had two sons. The younger one said to his father, 'Father, give me my share of the estate.' So he divided his property between them.

"Not long after that, the younger son got together all he had, set off for a distant country and there squandered his wealth in wild living After he had spent everything, there was a severe famine in that whole country, and he began to be in need. So he went and hired himself out to a citizen of that country, who sent him to his fields to feed pigs. He longed to fill his stomach with the pods that the pigs were eating, but no one gave him anything.

"When he came to his senses, he said, 'How many of my father's hired servants have food to spare, and here I am starving to death! So I will set out and go back to my father and say to him: Father, I have sinned against heaven and against you. I am no longer worthy to be called your son; make me like one of your hired servants. So he got up and went to his father.

"But while he was still a long way off, his father saw him and was filled with compassion for him; he ran to his son, threw his arms around him and kissed him.

"The son said to him, 'Father, I have sinned against heaven and against you. I am no longer worthy to be called your son.'

"But the father said to his servants, 'Quick! Bring the best robe and put it on him. Put a ring on his finger and sandals on his feet Bring the fattened calf and kill it. Let's have a feast and celebrate. For this son of mine was dead and is alive again; he was lost and is found.' So they began to celebrate.

"Meanwhile, the older son was in the field. When he came near the house, he heard music and dancing So he called one of the servants and asked him what was going on. 'Your brother has come,' he replied, 'and your father has killed the fattened calf because he has him back safe and sound.'

"The older brother became angry and refused to go in. So his father went out and pleaded with him. But he answered his father, 'Look! All these years I've been slaving for you and never disobeyed your orders. Yet you never gave me even a young goat so I could celebrate with my friends. But when this son of yours who has squandered your property with prostitutes comes home, you kill the fattened calf for him!'

"'My son,' the father said, 'you are always with me, and everything I have is yours. But we had to celebrate and be glad, because this brother of yours was dead and is alive again; he was lost and is found.'"

The first question the story may raise for the readers is, "Am I lost?" The father in the story is our heavenly Father, God, who patiently waits for us to return to Him with a humble heart. He does not dwell on our past but offers us everything in His kingdom.

Nothing is spared, we get it all. The best of the best. The older son is bitter and resentful. This blinds him from seeing the treasures that are all around him already. Do we get complacent about God's salvation that we already have? Do we show resentment for sinners going to heaven when they wait until their deathbed to repent and accept God as their Savior?

This highlights the fact that even though we may stray from Him, He is jubilant when we come back. Never feel like you have done so much that you will not be welcome. **Everyone** is welcome in God's eyes and in His kingdom. When we are welcomed back and start the relationship with Him, does that make us perfect or better than others. No.

A lot of people think of Christianity as behavior modification. You attend church regularly and start acting like other Christians. From a man's perspective, if we learn the information needed, we can "man up," change our behaviors and become more spiritual through our determination to get better. That may work for a while but is not the long-term answer. It is too easy to slip back into our past behaviors. I am so glad I have a forgiving God who welcomes me back regardless of my behavior if I ask for forgiveness.

So many children attend church with their parents growing up, bond with other classmates in Sunday School, and get confirmed in the church. In my church, as well as other denominations, they hold confirmation classes for those around the age of 14. You learn more in-depth information about the church and the beliefs of Christianity. Your confirmation is when you officially join the church and confirm your faith in Jesus Christ as your Lord and Savior.

Too often, when you graduate from high school and move off on your own to college or your career, going to church is no longer a habit that you continue. It is not that you forget about God, but you are not acknowledging Him regularly. You get distracted by this newfound "freedom." You can sleep in on Sunday morning since you were out late Saturday night. The church would get in the way of that. Maybe you moved to a new town and did not bother finding a church to attend.

Eventually, you graduate from college, get settled in your career, possibly get married, and have children. Significantly, the part about having kids gets you thinking about church again. You remember how your parents took you to church regularly and how it impacted on your life. You decide that you want that for your kids as well. You start attending church and make it an intentional habit. But does this bring you closer to God?

It becomes very frustrating to figure out that determination is not a strategy. You were determined to go to church and become a better Christian. To have a closer relationship with God. Christianity is heart transformation, not behavior transformation. It all starts with the heart. We cannot take a "fake it until you make it" mentality. We see this in so many aspects of our lives. To succeed, you must have something inside you, a total belief and ownership of the situation or plan.

> *The good man brings good things out of the good stored up in his heart, and the evil man brings evil things out of the evil stored up in his heart. For out of the overflow of his heart his mouth speaks.* (Luke 6:45)

Your genuine faith is what resides in your heart. I am not saying behavior is unimportant; it does not start there. Your behaviors will follow your heart. What is the best way to describe the faith in your heart? Be honest with yourself. What kind of relationship do you have with God? Think about what changed your heart and your faith. What was that moment, or did it slowly build over the years?

Developing a heart for God is essential for a life of faith. It requires us to cultivate certain qualities and behaviors to grow in our relationship with Him. It involves being intentional about the choices we make and the actions we take so that our hearts are aligned with His will. We want to delve into how we can cultivate a relationship with God and make our faith stronger. Developing a heart for God is not as difficult as it may sound. Your behaviors do play a factor in where your heart is led. Going to church and fellowshipping with other Christians leads you to understand what God wants from you and where He directs you. It involves concerning our hearts with the concerns of God's heart. We must develop those qualities that are worth having in our lives. We need to open our hearts to God to work within us.

Think about what you think about most. Are more of your thoughts about what you will eat next, or about sports or another person? It has been said that whatever consumes our thoughts is our idol. It is easy to forget that God is always with us, in our lives and in our thoughts. We often get so caught up in our own lives that we forget to take a moment to think about Him. However, it is important to remember that He should consume our thoughts and be a part of everything we do. By taking the time to reflect on His presence, we can develop a deeper understanding of His love and grace for us. This realization can bring about peace and joy in our lives as we strive to live according to His will. How much of your time is spent thinking about God in your life?

Consider how you spend your money. The Bible says, "Where your treasure is, there your heart will be also." Do you spend your money only on yourself? Remember, when the Bible speaks of tithing, it's not about God needing our money. It's a gentle reminder that what truly matters to Him is the condition of our hearts. Giving generously allows us to cultivate a spirit of gratitude and generosity, drawing closer to God in the process. It's a universal truth that our hearts follow our money. We have the power to shape our priorities and passions through the way we spend and invest. Let's choose wisely and let our hearts be guided toward what truly matters to us.

So, now that we know we need to turn our hearts to God to have a relationship with Him fully, what does that look like? Reading the book of 1 John, we see many tests to determine whether our faith is genuine. A truly converted person will have a growing sensitivity to and turning from sin. 1 John 1:5-10 *This is the message we have heard from him and declare to you: God is light; in him there is no darkness at all. If we claim to have fellowship with him and yet walk in the darkness, we lie and do not live out the truth. But if we walk in the light, as he is in the light, we have fellowship with one another, and the blood of Jesus, his Son, purifies us from all sin. If we claim to be without sin, we deceive ourselves and the truth is not in us. If we confess our sins, he is faithful and just and will forgive us our sins and purify us from all unrighteousness. If we claim we have not sinned, we make him out to be a liar and his word is not in us.*

He will grow in obedience to Christ and love for His people. He will have a growing knowledge of and love for God's truth as revealed in His Word. 1 John 2:21-27 says *So I am writing to you not because you don't know the truth but because you know the difference between truth and lies. And who is a liar? Anyone who says that Jesus is not the Christ. Anyone who denies the Father and the Son is an antichrist. Anyone who denies the Son doesn't have the Father, either. But anyone who acknowledges the Son has the Father also. So you must remain faithful to what you have been taught from the beginning. If you do, you will remain in fellowship with the Son and with the Father. And in this fellowship we enjoy the eternal life he promised us. I am writing these things to warn you about those who want to lead you astray. But you have received the Holy Spirit, and he lives within you, so you don't need anyone to teach you what is true. For the Spirit teaches you everything you need to know, and what he teaches is true—it is not a lie. So just as he has taught you, remain in fellowship with Christ.*

We strive for this fellowship with the Father, Son, and Holy Spirit. We turn our hearts to God and let Him work inside us through the Holy Spirit to change our hearts. It all starts with the heart. Before Pentecost, the Holy Spirit was not dwelling in the early Christians.

Note in 1 Samuel 16:13 *So as David stood there among his brothers, Samuel took the flask of olive oil he had brought and anointed David with the oil. And the Spirit of the Lord came powerfully upon David from that day on. Then Samuel returned to Ramah.* Before Pentecost, the Spirit of God did not permanently indwell all believers as He does in the present age of grace. Instead, He came upon certain ones to enable them to perform specific roles or tasks.

If you are truly converted, you have the Holy Spirit dwelling within you. The Holy Spirit will produce the fruit in you, as I will discuss in the following chapters about the Fruit of the Spirit. Galatians 5:16-23 *So I say, let the Holy Spirit guide your lives. Then you won't be doing what your sinful nature craves. The sinful nature wants to do evil, which is just the opposite of what the Spirit wants. And the Spirit gives us desires that are the opposite of what the sinful nature desires. These two forces are constantly fighting each other, so you are not free to carry out your good intentions. But when you are directed by the Spirit, you are not under obligation to the law of Moses. When you follow the desires of your sinful nature, the results are very clear: sexual immorality, impurity, lustful pleasures, idolatry, sorcery, hostility, quarreling, jealousy, outbursts of anger, selfish ambition, dissension, division, envy, drunkenness, wild parties, and other sins like these. Let me tell you again, as I have before, that anyone living that sort of life will not inherit the Kingdom of God. But the Holy Spirit produces this kind of fruit in our lives: love, joy, peace, patience, kindness, goodness, faithfulness, gentleness, and self-control. There is no law against these things!*

We all have the power to control our lives and improve them. But it all starts with the heart. When we open our hearts and minds to the Holy Spirit, we can find guidance for living a more fulfilling life. Being grateful for our gifts, being aware of what is happening around us, and opening our hearts to the guidance of the Holy Spirit can help us find peace and joy. With this awareness, we can be sure that our hearts lead us positively. How aware are you of the Holy Spirit working within you? How grateful are you to God for the gift of the Holy Spirit?

5

Fruit of the Spirit – Inward Traits

When we look at the Fruit of the Spirit, we can break them down into two categories. The first three, love, joy, and peace, are inward traits. Your emotions are something no one can take away from you; they're all yours; they come straight from your heart. Controlling our emotions can indeed be a challenging task. Still, it is reassuring to know that with the power of the Holy Spirit and inner strength, staying in control and channeling those feelings positively is always possible. Having faith in God's grace and relying on the guidance of the Holy Spirit can give us the necessary strength to navigate life's difficulties. When we trust in God's guidance, we recognize that every situation presents an opportunity for growth and learning. Even during challenging times, having faith allows us to see beyond immediate circumstances and find meaning in our experiences. The Holy Spirit is our source of wisdom, comfort, and empowerment. By placing our trust in God's grace while acknowledging the presence of the Holy Spirit within us, practicing self-awareness, seeking guidance through prayer, meditation, or similar practices, and cultivating a supportive community, we can work towards staying in control of our emotions and directing them in positive ways.

LOVE

> *"Anyone who does not love does not know God, because God is love."* 1 John 4:8 (ESV)

It sounds simple. Think about all the things and people you love. What comes to mind? The world overuses the word and idea of love to discuss material things like houses, clothes, food, and cars. We use the heart emoji to show that we love something. We love things that people do. We love the pictures people post or the creative things they make. People post photos and videos on social media to get attention and have people "love" them.

We then turn to love in our relationships. Maybe that is what the Bible is talking about. I see couples that have been married for over 50 years and the love and bond that they have together. I have to admit that I longed for this type of love. Though we all dream of a perfect romance, that is not what love is about. Love is not just emotions, romance, and a bouquet of flowers. To understand love, we must look at what love is to God.

God's love is all-encompassing, meaning there is no one He cannot or does not love for any reason. Read that again. God's love is all-encompassing, meaning there is **no one** He cannot or does not love for any reason. That is powerful but hard to comprehend. He loves everyone, with no exceptions. Because God loves us, we love others. We are called to love **all** people, not just our friends but even our enemies. That is where it gets complicated. Love our enemies? How do you do that?

Someone in your life has probably annoyed or upset you in some way and potentially did that for an extended period. Maybe there's someone whom you resent or even feel hatred toward? Almost everyone has those individuals around them at some point in their lives. Often, more than one person has caused us anger, hate, or resentment in the past.

Humans have feelings of hate. Sometimes it is short-lived, but other times it gets deep inside us, and we cannot let it go. It is often motivated by someone who has mistreated us or caused harm to us. In many verses, we are given direction, including Matthew 5:44, *"But I tell you, love your enemies and pray for those who persecute you."* First, to understand why Jesus said this, we must go further back into the Bible, to the Old Testament.

In ancient times, something was known as the Lex Talionis or the "law of retaliation." The basis of this form of law is the principle of proportionate punishment, often expressed under the motto "Let the punishment fit the crime," which particularly applies to mirror punishments (which may or may not be proportional). About torts, the Old Testament prescription "an eye for an eye" has often been interpreted, notably in Judaism, to mean equivalent monetary compensation, even to the exclusion of mirror punishment. In other cultures, notably Islam, the code has been taken more literally; a thief may lose his left hand as punishment. While Christianity has brought the possibility of forgiveness and mercy into the picture, the legal systems continue to prescribe punishments to fit the crimes that continue to be committed.

We may not be able to change the legal system or may not want to change the legal system due to the evil in our world and the fact that we cannot get everyone on the same page of loving each other. We can change, though, our approach. But even though revenge was rampant in the Old Testament times, a verse in Leviticus 19:18 states, *"Do not seek revenge or bear a grudge against anyone among your people."*

In the New Testament, Jesus is not presenting a new ethic. And he's not demanding something new. But instead, he's demanding more than most people were willing to do at the time. Demanding is a harsh word. That is like not taking no for an answer. Loving our neighbor is the second greatest commandment. Sadly, a couple of thousand years later, we still struggle to meet this demand.

Hating one another is the easy way out. To become more like our Savior, Jesus Christ, and live a life of faith and holiness, we must strive to nurture feelings of love, acceptance, and compassion. By harnessing these positive feelings within us, we can be sure that Christ's example of selflessness and kindness will guide us and help us draw nearer to Him. What does that look like? Show others genuine respect. Put yourself in their shoes. Try to understand what drives them and their beliefs. That does not mean you should agree with them. We need to know where they come from. What is the underlying reason for their attitude and actions? Accept them where they are. While you are on your path to a relationship with God and hopefully act accordingly, they may be in a different way that does not align with yours. That is okay.

Forgive them in your heart. Forgiveness doesn't mean you have to invite the person to dine at your table. It simply means moving on from the past. What happened in the past cannot be changed. Forgiveness is indeed a powerful act that can bring healing and growth. Instead, forgiveness allows you to release negative emotions and free yourself from the burden of resentment. By forgiving, you choose to let go of the past and move forward in your own life. It doesn't erase what happened or condone any wrongdoing; rather, it empowers you to focus on the present and future instead of dwelling on what cannot be changed. Holding onto anger and resentment can weigh us down emotionally, affecting our overall well-being. Accepting what has happened and choosing forgiveness enables personal growth and helps us find peace. Remember that forgiveness is a personal choice, and it may take time for some individuals to reach that point. It's important to prioritize your emotional well-being while navigating through this process.

Have you heard the phrase "kill them with kindness?" It is a saying that suggests responding to someone's negativity or hatred with kindness instead of matching their hostility. The idea behind this approach is that choosing to be kind can disrupt their expectations and potentially change the relationship dynamic. Responding to someone who dislikes you with kindness can catch them off guard and make them question their behavior. It may create a cognitive dissonance for them as they struggle to reconcile their negative feelings towards you with your positive attitude towards them. While this approach may not guarantee that they will start loving you or completely change their opinion about you, it can soften their feelings toward you. By consistently demonstrating kindness in response to hostility or negativity, it's possible to chip away at some of their animosity and create an opening for more positive interactions in the future.

Our love should imitate His love. In John 13:34-35, Jesus told his disciples to love one another as He loves them. He did not single out Judas, who He knew would soon betray Him and show him any less love than the rest of the disciples. No, He loved them all and expected us to do the same, even with those who betrayed us.

So, how do we love all people? Let us look at an example of seeds planted in a garden, like a parable in the Bible. Matthew 13: 22-24 says *The one who received the seed that fell among the thorns is the man who hears the word, but the worries of this life and the deceitfulness of wealth choke it, making it unfruitful. But the one who received the seed that fell on good soil is the man who hears the word and understands it. He produces a crop, yielding a hundred, sixty or thirty times what was sown." Jesus told them another parable: "The kingdom of heaven is like a man who sowed good seed in his field.* Just because the seed is planted does not mean that it will grow. It needs someone to care for it. We need to water it, fertilize it, ensure it gets enough sunlight, keep the weeds away, etc. It is the same thing with growing love in our hearts. It takes constant attention and nurturing. What must we do to help nurture the fruit the Holy Spirit wants to produce within us? It is much like tending a garden. First, you must clear out some things in your life so there is room for love to grow. It is like pulling weeds. Do you have hatred in your heart? Bitterness? Are you harboring any grudges? You must eliminate these things, or else love will have no room to grow.

Our country is very divided right now. Why is that? We are different. Some differences are political views, race (views explicitly on race), gender classification, sexuality, and gun control. We are not expected to agree with each other. God expects us to love one another. There were many examples in the Bible where Jesus loved the outcasts of society. Did He approve of everything they did? No, but He still loved them. Likewise, he does not approve of everything we do but still loves us.

I pray that God will break up the soil of our hearts and soften it so that the seeds of love will have an environment suitable for growth. Please help us to eliminate the weeds of hatred and negativity so they do not choke the ability of love to grow. Help us allow the Holy Spirit to work within us in developing a more profound love... a love like Christ's, which sees only the good in people. We realize that plants do not proliferate, and reaching maturity will take some time. Please give us the patience to continually grow and not give up on becoming more like Christ. The most essential quality is love.

Colossians 3:14 says *And above all these put on love, which binds everything together in perfect harmony.*

JOY

Jesus told His disciples, "These things I have spoken to you, that My joy may remain in you, and that your joy may be full" (John 15:11). Wouldn't you like to experience deep and enduring joy? Wouldn't you want to be joyful? You can.

The world struggles with a shortage of joy and an abundance of fear, worry, discouragement, and depression. Most people believe that the pursuit of pleasure is the key to happiness. However, research has shown that this pleasure-seeking often leads to short-term satisfaction but does not bring deep and lasting joy. This is because our brains are wired to seek out new experiences, which can lead to an obsessive need for more and more pleasure. This can result in a cycle of seeking pleasure without finding true happiness or contentment.

Let us first understand the difference between joy and happiness. Happiness is an emotion, and God never intended for people to be in that emotional state all the time. There is "a time to weep, and a time to laugh; a time to mourn, and a time to dance" (Ecclesiastes 3:4). We generally think of happiness as getting something. It is about us. But joy and happiness come much more from giving and serving than from getting.

The apostle Paul reminded his listeners that Jesus Christ had taught this very thing: "It is more blessed to give than to receive." (Acts 20:35). Giving to others and serving them will bring us joy.

Rejoice is the verb form of joy, meaning to feel or have joy! There is great emphasis in the Bible on feeling and expressing joy. That explains why the Bible also emphasizes prayers and songs that praise (celebrate) God. We glorify God when we go to church and joyfully sing Him songs and praises. Life can be full of joy, but it can also be full of things that steal our joy. From stressful jobs to illnesses, death of loved ones, economic strain, daily annoyances, and frustrations - all of these can challenge us and take away our sense of joy. So, how can we still find joy during all this chaos and uncertainty? One way is to practice self-care and take the time to do things we enjoy. Whether reading a book, listening to music, taking a walk outdoors, or engaging in a hobby that brings joy, these are all great ways to bring much-needed peace and happiness into our lives. The answer lies in learning to appreciate life's small moments and find ways to cope with our challenges. We can learn to accept that life will never be perfect and instead focus on what we have rather than what we don't have. Doing this brings us joy even when faced with difficult circumstances. It is a matter of changing our thinking. We can choose to be joyful! Think about everything God has done for you and thank Him for it. As the saying goes, "Count your blessings." Serve others and be an encouragement for them. It will bring you joy. If we truly believe what God has told us in the Bible, then we have plenty to rejoice about.

Absolute spiritual joy is the strength to forgive someone who has wronged you without holding a grudge or harboring any hatred towards them. You hope the person will eventually see the error of their ways and find peace in Heaven without hatred or animosity. To do this, you start with love. Matthew 22:39 says......." *Love your neighbor as yourself.*" So, we start with love, a powerful feeling that brings so much joy into our lives. This beautiful emotion can lift us up and make us feel alive, and the joy that it brings is simply incomparable. When love is present, everything else seems to fall into place, and the world can seem brighter.

> *"Joy is prayer; joy is strength: joy is love; joy is a net of love by which you can catch souls."*

MOTHER TERESA

PEACE

We continue in our discussion about the fruit of the Spirit. Peace is the third and final characteristic of our inward state mentioned in these verses. *But the fruit of the Spirit is love, joy, peace, patience, kindness, goodness, faithfulness, gentleness, and self-control; against such things there is no law.* Galatians 5:22-23

We often associate the concept of peace with the absence of chaos or struggles. The peace highlighted in this passage describes it as a feeling of tranquility or stillness rather than a lack of external turmoil. This inner peace is not driven by our environment or external factors but by the presence of the Holy Spirit. It is an internal feeling, an inner sense of calmness and serenity that resonates deep within our souls, providing us with peace and tranquility. It's a feeling that no external force can take away from us and serves as a beacon of hope in times of distress.

Peace is a state of tranquil and serene calmness, free from worry and stress, accompanied by an inner sense of contentment. As I journeyed through life, I realized that having faith in God's plans for me is paramount for success. I have found it to result from believing in an unseen power, trusting in His will, and relying on Him to get me through tough times. Having faith has been a major factor in how my life has turned out, helping me gain perspective and stay focused on what matters most. It is a beautiful blessing sent from Him that we can access through the power of the Holy Spirit. Even though the world is full of chaos and unrest, true peace remains untouched and cannot be taken away from us no matter what life throws at us. This peace resides deep within us and gives us the strength to find tranquility even in times of adversity.

In Philippians, the apostle Paul, locked in a depressing prison cell, wrote, "I have learned in whatever state I am to be content." He reminded his readers that they also could have "God's peace, which is far beyond human understanding." You, too, can have this unique contentment and peace!

We used to hear of someone being a nervous wreck or suffering a nervous breakdown. Emotions haven't changed, but how we describe them has. Tension, anxiety, depression, and panic attacks are today's standard designations. Finding peace in a contentious world can seem hopeless, but Scripture tells us to "seek peace and pursue it" (1 Peter 3:11).

To experience peace, you must take responsibility for your thoughts. Trust God's will...what he has in store for us...and what storms we may face along the way. He will carry us through them. With God's help, you can quit reacting with anger or self-pity. It is not your circumstances or other people determining your mood but your attitude towards them. We applied the same concept in pursuing joy in your life. These verses sum it up.

Do not be anxious about anything, but in every situation, by prayer and petition, with thanksgiving, present your requests to God. And the peace of God, which transcends all understanding, will guard your hearts and your minds in Christ Jesus. Philippians 4:6-7 (NIV)

When the stress of life starts to pile up, and it all feels too overwhelming, it's quite easy to become overwhelmed with anxiety, frustration, and a feeling like everything is spinning out of control. It's important during these times to take a step back and remember that even though things may seem tough, there is always a light at the end of the tunnel. In times of chaos and uncertainty, taking a few moments to pause and just be still can bring a sense of peace that is so refreshing - and that peace can often be attributed to the Holy Spirit that lives within us! This small interlude of stillness can help us realign our thoughts, allowing us to tackle our challenges better - all through the power of the Holy Spirit.

Peace is knowing that our God is in control. Peace is a state of tranquility or quietness of spirit that transcends circumstances.

That is different from saying everything will go how we want it to. The peace that surpasses all understanding comes from knowing that no matter what life throws at us, we can find joy in the assurance that our ultimate victory is found in Jesus Christ and not through any of our own abilities or circumstances. This deep, profound knowledge of understanding life and its intricacies brings a sense of comfort and security to the soul that transcends all worldly comprehension. It offers a unique perspective on life that cannot be obtained through any materialistic possessions or worldly pursuits. If we focus on our circumstances, our peace and joy will come and go like ocean waves. If we focus on Jesus, our circumstances no longer control our emotions. Reach out to Him with your worries, needs, cares, and concerns. He will always be there for you. When you surrender your worries and anxieties to God, you no longer have to carry the burden of the things that can rob you of your inner peace. Allowing Him to take over these worries and concerns can bring your life a newfound sense of peace, joy, and contentment.

In Matthew 8:23-27, we read about how Jesus calmed the storm.

Then Jesus got into the boat and started across the lake with his disciples. Suddenly, a fierce storm struck the lake, with waves breaking into the boat. But Jesus was sleeping. The disciples went and woke him up, shouting, "Lord, save us! We're going to drown!"

Jesus responded, "Why are you afraid? You have so little faith!" Then he got up and rebuked the wind and waves, and suddenly there was a great calm. The disciples were amazed. "Who is this man?" they asked. "Even the winds and waves obey him!"

The disciples were afraid of what was going to happen to them when they did not have control of the situation. They could not control the storm and were probably thinking about the worst-case scenario. What if they perished in the storm? Do we start thinking that way in our circumstances? What is the worst-case scenario? How can we ever get through it? But what was Jesus' response? He asked them why they were afraid, implying that if they had faith in Him, there was nothing to fear. This is the same with us. If we have faith in Him, we have nothing to fear. If He can calm the storms, our circumstances are minute in comparison. We need faith.

6

Fruit of the Spirit - Outward Traits

In the last chapter, we examined the inner traits of the fruit of the Spirit. Now it is time to take a closer look at the external manifestation of these spiritual gifts that are developed when we allow our hearts and minds to be filled with His presence. These outward traits are evidence that the Holy Spirit is within us, guiding us in our daily lives and helping us to grow in spirit as He works through us and reveals Himself in our behavior.

PATIENCE

Patience is the next fruit in the passage. You have probably heard the phrase; Patience is a virtue. With everything going on these past couple of years, with everything going on with Covid, we have had to learn to be patient. We like to be active and social but had to patiently wait at home until "the coast was clear" to start getting out in public again. We had to patiently wait for a vaccine to be produced and then, in the beginning, patiently wait in long lines to get the vaccine. As you could tell from the political bantering back and forth, some people had no patience.

Nowadays, we have become so accustomed to the idea of instant gratification that we often forget to find satisfaction in hard work and dedication. This false sense of convenience has slowly eroded our ability to work through difficult tasks and persevere through challenging situations. While this can be a blessing in some ways, it also has the potential to take away from the learning experience of delayed gratification - something that is a valuable skill to have in life. The Bible is filled with stories and examples of why waiting and being patient is important. From the story of Joseph in the Old Testament to Jesus's teachings in the New Testament, we can learn valuable lessons about why we should exercise patience when dealing with difficult situations.

The Bible teaches us that waiting and being patient can bring about positive results in our lives. It tells us to trust in God's timing and plan for our lives, no matter how hard it may seem. The Israelites spending 40 years in the wilderness waiting for God's promise of the promised land is a great example. We can learn from these stories that God's timing is perfect and that if we trust in Him, He will provide us with what we need at the right time. By looking back at these Bible examples, we can better understand why waiting and being patient is so important.

Rejoice in hope, be patient in tribulation, be constant in prayer. Romans 12:12 (ESV)

It's important to stay hopeful, be patient, and remember to pray in difficult times. This verse encourages us to look for joy and hope even in difficult times and to stay connected with God through prayer. It reminds us that no matter what we are going through, we can still find peace and strength if we turn our eyes toward God.

We have talked about rejoicing (Joy) as one of the fruit of the Spirit. We gain peace through our communication (prayer) with God. The Holy Spirit is the great provider of all the fruit. We see how they all tie in together. It is that peace that God is in control, even in tribulations, which give us the peace and patience to wait it out. Wait until His will is fulfilled, and we reap the benefits.

> *And let us not grow weary of doing good, for in due season we will reap, if we do not give up.*
> Galatians 6:9 (ESV)

This is one of my favorite verses. I have witnessed others approaching business with different values than I have applied in my career. I have been in the food service business for four decades. In several cases, I have seen them be successful (by society's standards), while I have been disappointed by not making as much money or having a higher position. I did not have patience early in my career and paid the price. I learned (the hard way) that putting a career above family and trying to get ahead quickly without analyzing the costs is a recipe for failure.

As I recommitted my loyalty to God to oversee my life and truly believe in His will, a sense of peace came over me. This was in 2008. I have seen the fruit of the Spirit grow within me since then. I live stress-free. I think my "due season" has come, and I am reaping the benefits of my faithfulness. My career took an unexpected turn in 2008, and I love my job more than ever. I give all the credit to God. I allowed Him to take over. Shortly after that, a new position with my current employer took me out of the traditional path up the corporate ladder and sent me down a different road utilizing other talents of mine.

Trust in the Lord. Open your communication with Him through

prayer and let the Holy Spirit work within you. You will see the fruit develop within you, how it affects your surroundings, and how you feel about it.

KINDNESS AND GOODNESS

The following two fruit of the Spirit are related in nature. Kindness and Goodness. The Holy Spirit works in us and through us to grow this fruit.

> *But the fruit of the Spirit is love, joy, peace, patience, kindness, goodness, faithfulness, gentleness, self-control; against such things there is no law.*
> Galatians 5:22-23

All nine of these fruit are attributes of God that He wants us to experience in our own lives and actions. He has given us the Holy Spirit to grow these within us. When you think of kindness, what comes to mind? Is kindness a way to describe how you should treat others? We should be kind to one another. The dictionary meaning of kindness is the quality of being friendly, generous, and considerate. Is this kindness? Is it just being nice to someone or giving them what they want? I know someone good at customer service but admits that sometimes she is being fake in her kindness. I see that approach as being nice to someone else. Kindness might include tough love. It is caring about what is best for the person.

We benefit from being kind as well as the person we are kind to. Proverbs 11:17 tells us that a man who is kind benefits himself, but a cruel man hurts himself. Think about this. Kindness not only makes others happy. It uplifts our spirit too.

If that is kindness, what is goodness? In movies, we have battles of good versus evil. Is good the opposite of evil? How does it compare to kindness? Kindness is passive in how it flows between people. Goodness is more aggressive. It is the act of doing good, not just a feeling passed on. Goodness is the action that comes from having the Holy Spirit within you. These actions are for the benefit of others. Goodness comes from God. James 1:17 says, "Every good and perfect gift is from above, coming down from the Father of the heavenly lights." In letting the Holy Spirit control us, we are blessed with the fruit of goodness.

Goodness is doing what is right, even when it is not easy. Goodness is a choice and an action. To show goodness, you must decide to be good and do the right thing purposefully. Think about that for a minute. Goodness is doing what is right, even when it is not easy. Too often, we take the easy path. How is God good? In his commentary on Psalm 46, Charles Spurgeon wrote that God is good — not because he causes things that seem or feel "good" to happen in our lives, but because God comes closer to us during the storm than the storm could ever be.

We can say that God is good no matter how bad the storm is, how much pain we experience, or how different the outcome is from what we have prayed for. In life's most challenging moments, God comes close to us and does not change, falter, quit, leave, or let go.

"God is good all the time. All the time, God is good."

Let the Holy Spirit work inside you so you can be kind and good "all the time."

FAITHFULNESS

Faithfulness comes from a place of trust and loyalty. Hebrews 11:1 says, "Now faith is a confidence in what we hope for and assurance about what we do not see." Faithfulness requires us to submit our ways to God. It comes from realizing that we need a Savior, and He controls our lives. If we are full of faithfulness, we believe in God; we trust that He always has our best interests at heart.

As we grow the fruit of the Spirit in our hearts and lives, they build on each other. When we are faithful, it gives us peace, patience, and joy. This translates into how we treat others with kindness and goodness. As these other traits grow, so does our faithfulness.

Is it much easier to be faithful when everything is going our way? When things go wrong, do we lose our faith in God? I do not believe this is necessarily true. When everything goes our way, we tend to forget about God and take much credit for what is going on as what we have done. We do not stop to give Him thanks for what He has done. When things go wrong, we turn to God more. We turn to Him, looking for direction and comfort. We would not do that if we did not have faith that He would come through for us.

In our spiritual walk, we will have doubts and fears and wonder if God is not there. Maybe He is not as good as He says He is. There will be so many terrifying "maybes" throughout life. Unfortunately, there is a misunderstanding that doubt and fear mean we failed and should feel ashamed. But guess what? Even "Doubting Thomas," looking right at the risen Lord but did not know what to think, was treated with grace and patience by Jesus so he could grow in his faith and understanding.

God has always been faithful to us. Through the Holy Spirit, we are growing fruit (the traits of God that develop in us). As we grow in our faith, we strive to be more Christ-like. This is accomplished through the Holy Spirit working within us. God is always faithful to us. Therefore, we need always to be faithful to Him.

GENTLENESS

The next fruit is gentleness. We often think of gentleness as tenderness or even softness. Dictionary definitions say it is the quality of being kind, tender, or mild-mannered. But is that how the Bible describes it? It can be described as having a humble heart and being kind toward others. Matthew 11:29 says *"Take my yoke upon you and learn from me, for I am gentle and humble in heart, and you will find rest for your souls."*

This tells us to learn how to be gentle and humble in our hearts. We will find rest for our souls. One way to be gentle is to accept the hardships He allows in our lives, considering them helpful for our spiritual development. When we accept the hardships, it will give us rest. It will provide us with peace.

> *"A soft answer turns away wrath, but a harsh word stirs up anger."* Proverbs 15:1 (ESV)

Jesus' life reminds us that sometimes silence, acceptance, and gentleness are the strongest actions. It is the humble and meek attitude of wanting to help other people instead of wanting to be superior to them. This attitude flows from a spirit of genuine love for the individual—having valid, outgoing concern for their well-being.

In John 8:1-11 we read about the scribes and the Pharisees wanting to stone a woman to death for adultery. They said to him, "Teacher, this woman has been caught in the act of adultery. Now in the Law Moses commanded us to stone such women. So what do you say?" His response was "And as they continued to ask him, he stood up and said to them, "Let him who is without sin among you be the first to throw a stone at her." They all left. Did Jesus condone her sins? No. He was gentle in His approach. Jesus stood up and said to her, "Woman, where are they? Has no one condemned you?" She said, "No one, Lord." And Jesus said, "Neither do I condemn you; go, and from now on sin no more."

We must strive to be more like Jesus and be gentle in our

approach to all situations. That includes times when we strongly disagree with what is taking place. I cannot help to think about the protests in recent years and how much of an impact it makes when peaceful compared to aggressive behaviors. When you are bold, the opposition will fight back, making things worse. You can be strong in your convictions but gentle in presenting them.

Thank you, Lord, for your gentleness as we continue to sin. Through the Holy Spirit, grow the seed of gentleness in us. Please help us to understand that gentleness is not a weakness but a strength. Teach us how to be humble in our hearts. A humble heart values the welfare of others ahead of its own. There is so much we can learn from you. Open our hearts and minds to learn and apply your traits to our lives. Amen.

SELF-CONTROL

The last fruit of the Spirit is self-control. When we receive the Holy Spirit, the seed is planted. The seed will eventually grow into fruit in the right environment. We need to nourish it by growing closer to God.

> *But the fruit of the Spirit is love, joy, peace, patience, kindness, goodness, faithfulness, gentleness, self-control; against such things there is no law.* Galatians 5:22-23 (ESV)

There are many things we cannot control. For example, we cannot control the weather even though we would love to. Do you know people that are control freaks? A control freak feels an obsessive need to exercise control over themselves and others and take command of any situation.

It is sometimes surprising how little control we have over other people—even in our families and our children. Parents are often shocked by their children's behavior, especially by their teenagers, whom they thought they had trained well. Many parents have discovered that merely telling their children what they can or cannot do—accompanied by warnings of dire punishment—is not enough to control their behavior when the children are under the pressure of a situation.

Ironically, we want to control others but fail to have as much control over ourselves as we need. Please think of the habits or addictions we have developed over the years that are detrimental to our success and lives. We see an excellent example of self-control implied in Proverbs 25:28: "Whoever has no rule over his own spirit is like a city broken down, without walls."

Self-control helps us to resist temptation and avoid conforming to the things of this world. It guides our decisions and correlates with how we show the other fruit in our lives. It is how we respond to situations as compared to reacting to situations. When we react, our emotions jump in and take over. Self-control allows us to think through the problem and respond more Christ-like.

Self-control is not the ability to decide what we think is best for us but the power to determine what God feels is best for us. We may think we know what is best for us, but I continue to look back and realize I had no clue. That may be a little harsh, but I see where my decisions took me down the wrong path, and when I let God make the decisions for me, the results were far better.

As I wrapped up this series, I reflected on how I started the process. I would accidentally call them the fruits of the Spirit (plural). They are all one fruit, a package deal. They are all intertwined. It is the essence of God—His character. Even though we can expect to fall short of what He wants us to be, we should not accept falling short. Instead, we need to strive to be more and more like Him.

No sins or disobedience are done when we exhibit this fruit.

Imagine a world where everyone exhibits these traits in all aspects of their lives. We would not need any laws. No one would ever need to be punished for what they did. Since the temptation of the flesh exists, this world will never exist. We may be the seed of the fruit of the Spirit. The Holy Spirit planted a seed in us to grow into fruit, and we are, in turn, the seed being planted in this world so it can grow and influence those around us. Imagine a world if enough of us, as seeds of the fruit of the Spirit, made a difference. We could change the world. That sounds like a great goal to me. So join me in developing the fruit of the Spirit within you and exhibiting it in your lives to make this world a better place. More Christ-like.

7

The struggle is real

There are different ways we struggle in life. We are very "routine" oriented as humans. We do not like change, and we enjoy being able to plan and everything working out as we planned it. But how often does that work for you? Does God's plan work out the way we want it to? Are we even aware of how working His plan in our lives, even though we struggle at times? I had a discussion with a coworker about the unplanned career detours, relationship changes in our lives, and God's role in them.

We do not ask or desire for jobs to be ended unexpectedly, for relationships to fail, or for other harmful things to happen. Instead, looking back at the outcome after these events, we see how God orchestrated them and provided an abundance of blessings afterward. That got me thinking about all the people I have read about in the bible. I need help to think of one person whose life went exactly as planned. There were none who did not experience some struggle in their life. However, I can tell you about many people who struggled, let God direct their path, and were blessed beyond belief because they trusted God.

The first person who comes to mind is Job. He was a devout Christian doing everything right in God's eyes, but he still had to suffer. I will discuss Job in a future chapter. In 1 Peter 5:10, we can see how we should expect to suffer before becoming strong.

> *In his kindness God called you to share in his eternal glory by means of Christ Jesus. So after you have suffered a little while, he will restore, support, and strengthen you, and he will place you on a firm foundation.*

But why do we have to suffer? What is the purpose? We often ask, "Why me, Lord? Why me?". When God makes us suffer, He asks us to submit to Him, to come to Him, and stop fighting Him. He is helping us remember that we don't have to walk this life alone because He is our Father. There is goodness in suffering because it gives us blessings; we can receive no other way.

In this conversation over dinner with a coworker, we talked about job opportunities that came about because of God working His plan instead of us working ours. We would not choose to lose our job due to budget cutbacks. We would want a job lined up before leaving one. Also, we would not just end a career unexpectedly that we enjoyed. But by God allowing us to lose our job and complete our relationships, it opened our minds to see other opportunities. These opportunities are the path to a new and better career—a new relationship.

God has an incredible sense of vision of what possibilities are out there. We cannot even imagine most of them. But our first thought is not about what God wants to do with our lives. Instead, we desire to pursue our dreams, our "vision," and then ask Him to bless it. How can we tell when it is His vision compared to ours? First, let's define what we mean by a vision. A vision is something that prompts an action. It is motivating. Vision evokes awe and imagination. What can the future hold? Vision builds off purpose. Purpose gives meaning to your efforts. Have you asked yourself, "What is my purpose in life?" If you knew you would not fail, what would you do for God's glory in your lifetime? How is God speaking to you and directing your vision? Is He showing you His vision and asking you to "buy into it? He puts things in motion to eventually come together to fulfill His will in our lives. Who is God shaping you to be? What does He want to accomplish through you?

He wants us to lean on Him, to depend on Him. We need to realize we cannot do it alone; we do not have to do it alone. We need to put our trust in Him. That is not easy, but it is possible. Open your heart and mind to the endless possibilities for our future and the blessings God can bestow on us if we let Him.

So how do we determine God's purpose for us? What is His vision? Think about what Bible verses have spoken to you over the years. Which ones resonated and made an impact on you? Do they have a common theme? Why were they necessary? They may have offered hope, given you direction, or forged your identity.

> *"For by grace you have been saved through faith, and this is not your own doing; it is the gift of God—not the result of works, so that no one may boast. For we are what he has made us, created in Christ Jesus for good works, which God prepared beforehand to be our way of life."*
> Ephesians 2:8-10

God made us for good works. He has prepared beforehand. God is not acting day to day. He has our whole life already scripted. When you become a Christian, you set yourself on a path to become more Christlike. But have you thought about what all that may entail?

> *"To this you were called, because Christ suffered for you, leaving you an example that you should follow in his steps." -* 1 Peter 2:21

Jesus went through the ultimate suffering. He was put to death on the cross. For you and me! That puts it all into perspective. We do not know what suffering is.

We talk about our struggles with our circumstances and how things do not go our way. But there are other struggles in our lives. Everyone struggles to be Christlike. Even Paul struggled as he wrote about in Romans. In these verses, Paul talks about his battle with sin. We can all relate to this.

> *So the trouble is not with the law, for it is spiritual and good. The trouble is with me, for I am all too human, a slave to sin. I don't really understand myself, for I want to do what is right, but I don't do it. Instead, I do what I hate.* Romans 7:14-15

Aren't we all too human and enslaved people to sin? We must overcome this in our path to a closer relationship with God. We cannot do it alone. We need God's love and support. That is precisely what He wants from us. He wants us to rely on Him for this love and support.

These struggles we experience are just setbacks. With the right attitude, you can get back on track. When you hit a setback, it's okay to tell God you're mad, sad, or depressed. It's okay to express all your emotions to God. Just don't be resentful. When you are resentful, it is saying you don't trust God when troubles hit. It's like a poison that will tear your life apart if you let it. Job did not become bitter or resentful for everything happening to him. He endured so much but always was aware of the big picture. He trusted God. He knew God was in control even when it seemed everything was falling apart around him.

> *And he said, "Naked I came from my mother's womb, and naked shall I return. The Lord gave, and the Lord has taken away; blessed be the name of the Lord." Job 1:21 (ESV)*

Faith is indeed often tested throughout our lives. It can be challenging to fully trust Him to protect and guide us through difficult times, especially in the early stages of our relationship with God. Trust is a virtue that takes time to develop as we experience setbacks and reflect on how they fit into God's plan for us. Each setback we overcome can strengthen our faith and increase our confidence in surrendering control of our circumstances to Him.

In life's journey, God often uses trials and suffering to shape and build our character. During these times of difficulty, we are tested, refined, and strengthened. Just as a sculptor molds clay into a beautiful masterpiece, God uses our trials to mold us into the person He has designed us to be. We learn important lessons about perseverance, resilience, and faith through the challenges we face.

Suffering may seem unbearable now, but through these experiences, we grow in character. During our darkest moments, we discover our true strength and find solace in knowing that God is with us every step of the way. Instead of viewing suffering as a punishment or a sign of God's absence, let us embrace it as an opportunity for growth. Let us trust in His plan for our lives and believe He will use every trial to shape us into better versions of ourselves. Remember, your character is not built in times of ease but in moments of struggle. Embrace the challenges with open arms and allow God to mold you into the person He has destined you to become.

8

Can you hear me now?

God is continually attempting to capture and sustain our attention. However, it remains crucial for us to listen and pay heed to these messages actively. God communicates with us through various means, such as through scripture, prayer, nature, and even through other people. The important thing is for us to be open and receptive to these messages and actively listen to what God might be trying to communicate to us. We can deepen our understanding of ourselves and our relationship with Him by paying heed and being attentive. He spoke to Adam in the garden. Noah was instructed to build an ark. He spoke to Moses in a burning bush. He promised Abraham a son. Paul heard His voice on the way to Damascus. But does God still speak to us today? If so, how? When? Where?

Often, when people ask this question, they talk about an audible voice. And God can do that. He can do anything He wants. He's God. Why, then, don't I hear His voice? Am I not good enough? Are there too many people in the world today for Him to speak to all of us? God uses many ways to talk to us, and each of us "hears" Him differently.

We have been provided His Word, the Scriptures, so He can speak to us through them. I can read the same verses for years, and then it really "speaks" to me one day. It was just the right words I needed to hear at that moment. Or I am sitting in the pew at church, and the sermon seems to be calling me out. This is my Lord talking to me. Earlier this year, we had a guest pastor. He was the pastor of our church for about six years (in the past), and everyone loved him. The parishioners who had been around since he was the pastor were excited to have him return, even for one Sunday. When he started his sermon, he said that initially, he was preparing to give a sermon about the start of the new year and fresh beginnings but decided to preach on "God's Tear Bottle" at the last minute.

David wrote while in the custody of his enemies, "You have kept count of my tossings; put my tears in your bottle" (Psalm 56:8, ESV). David was going through a difficult time. The idea behind the keeping of "tears in a bottle" is remembrance. David is expressing a deep trust in God—God will remember his sorrow and tears and will not forget about him. David is confident that God is on his side. He says, during this troubling time, "This I know, God is for me" (Psalm 56:9, ESV) There are many times where we shed tears. I was sitting with a dear friend who had recently lost her son to a sudden cardiac arrest. This sermon was exactly what she needed then, and coming from a pastor/friend made it more special. God was speaking to her from the pulpit. The pastor was not aware of her situation. He had not changed his sermon for her. God directed him to change the sermon.

God may use a friend, a teacher, a parent, or a preacher to convey His message of truth to us. Their words may be a warning, a blessing, or prophetic truth about our lives. Whether we choose to hear it or ignore it depends on us. Words from a speaker or Christian author have challenged and sometimes convicted me. These things may not strike you as "hearing" God's voice, but we tend to think of God in our terms. He is more significant than that. He once spoke through a donkey (Numbers 22:28). Why then, can't He speak through anyone at any time or in any way He wants to?

I was asked to speak to senior citizens about living stress-free. I had just written a stress management book and taught myself to live stress-free. But what do I say to a group of seniors? I plotted out my speech and practiced it numerous times to be prepared. I filled out index cards with an outline of the speech so I could refer to them if I got stuck to get back on track. Partway through the speech, I got sidetracked and went in a different direction with the approach. After I finished, I looked at the notes and realized I had given quite a different speech than what was prepared. After lunch, a lady approached me and told me that my words were exactly what she needed to hear that day. She had been struggling at home, and I gave her comfort. Later, her pastor told me that the lady was suffering from emotional abuse from her kids. God gave me the words that day for Him to speak to her through me.

The New Testament was the fulfillment of God's special plan. First, it's the gospel: the good news of Jesus Christ. *"In the past God spoke to our forefathers through the prophets at many times and in various ways, but in these last days he has spoken to us by His Son, whom he appointed heir of all things, and through whom he made the universe"* Hebrews 1:1-2, NIV). Through the words of Jesus in Scripture, we can "hear" God's heart and God's voice–and know what God is truly like. Comparing us to sheep and Him as the Shepherd, Jesus says in John 10:27, NKJV: "My sheep hear my voice, and I know them, and they follow me." Why? Because the sheep know who He is. They belong to Him, and they recognize Him by the sound of His voice. And He's the one who will always lovingly lead them on the right path–again and again.

The divine Spirit within us constantly communicates through our conscience, guiding us toward making the right decisions in life's intricate web. It serves as a gentle reminder, urging us to stay on the path of righteousness even when temptation lingers nearby. The question is, do we take heed of this sacred wisdom and listen to its compelling call? In these moments of choice, we truly define our character and embrace the true power that lies within us. Let us open our hearts and minds to the divine wisdom bestowed upon us, for it is through listening and following this inner voice that we embark on a journey toward greatness and fulfillment. Do we listen?

God speaks to us through nature—His creation.

> "Look at the birds of the air: they neither sow nor reap nor gather into barns, and yet your heavenly Father feeds them. Are you not of more value than they? And which of you by being anxious can add a single hour to his span of life?
>
> And why are you anxious about clothing? Consider the lilies of the field, how they grow: they neither toil nor spin, yet I tell you, even Solomon in all his glory was not arrayed like one of these. But if God so clothes the grass of the field, which today is alive and tomorrow is thrown into the oven, will he not much more clothe you, O you of little faith?"
>
> Matthew 6:26-30

God can use even ants to communicate with you. He did that in Proverbs 6:6-9. "Take a lesson from the ants, ... Learn from their ways and be wise! For though they have no king to make them work, yet they labor hard all summer, gathering food for the winter." If you're sensitive enough, you'll hear God speaking through means we often ignore. Birds flying in the hair should remind us of how God can provide our needs. Though the flowers are beautiful, they do not last. This may be God communicating that nothing is permanent.

We're told in Psalm 19:1-6 that, 'The heavens declare the glory of God; the skies proclaim the work or His hands. Day after day they pour forth speech; night after night they display knowledge. There is no speech or language where their voice is not heard. Their voice goes out into all the earth, their words to the ends of the world.'

God speaks to you through His word, His Holy Spirit, and many other ways. But you're responsible for tuning in and learning how to hear Him. We see this throughout the Bible.

> *Behold, I stand at the door and knock. If anyone hears my voice and opens the door, I will come in to him and eat with him, and he with me.*
> Revelation 3:20 (ESV)

> *Incline your ear, and come to me; hear, that your soul may live; and I will make with you an everlasting covenant, my steadfast, sure love for David.*
> Isaiah 55:3 (ESV)

> *You shall walk after the Lord your God and fear him and keep his commandments and obey his voice, and you shall serve him and hold fast to him.*
> Deuteronomy 13:4 (ESV)

Too often, our lives get so busy and "noisy" with all the activities. These things hinder our ability to hear God's voice. It gets where God's quiet voice is nearly undetectable. At that point, we need to pause and set some time aside to pray, focus on Him, and listen. It takes faith to hear God's voice. When we are quiet before the Lord, we can hear from Him more clearly. Spending time in His Word, God speaks to you. You can listen to God speak to you in worship, through music, and through quiet times, we wait on him to speak, and if he talks, then we listen. Half of communication is listening.

9

Confiding in a friend

Do you have that one friend whom you confide in? The one you can tell your deepest secrets and know they will keep them private? Confiding in someone represents two people pressing or leaning together in quiet conversation, a posture that friends take when they share confidence between them. They tell each other secrets and know that they will stay confidential. Psalms 25:14 (NIV) says *"The LORD confides in those who fear him; he makes his covenant known to them."* It initially suggests intimate friendship, then that God opens His mind to those who fear Him so that He can more carefully instruct them in His way and will.

As you develop your relationship with God, you will build on the relationship over time just as you would with your friends. It does not escalate to this level immediately. It builds over time. God already knows what is on your mind, so it is not like you have secrets that He doesn't already know. The difference is your attitude towards those "secrets". Do you share them in your prayers, in your confessions? Are there things you are ashamed of that you do not want to discuss with others, let alone God?

So far, we are talking about confiding in Him. But this bible verse talks about God confiding in us. That is a whole different approach. What would He be confiding in us about? It says He will open our minds. This gives Him the opening to instruct us, and we pay attention to His will and instructions for us. He will provide us with guidance. He is not putting this information on social media for all to know what He is telling us. No. He is confiding in just you and me individually. Now it is up to us to listen and follow that guidance.

God seeks the seeker who says, "I want to know you. Reveal yourself to me, please. Show me the truth, Your truth. Give me eyes to see you and ears to hear you." He is drawn to the humble heart that comes with offerings in both hands: a confession of ignorance and a thirst for the real God in the other. God doesn't reveal Himself only to the spiritually mature or the theologically perfect.

God confides in His little ones, His children. It is all about the relationship and not about knowledge. Just what does it mean that "God confides" in someone? It means the same thing you think of where your best friend is concerned. Picture two souls sitting close together on a couch, pouring their thoughts and concerns into one another. Or think of a child snuggled close to a mother or father, always presuming upon the right to lean intimately into them, confident of their love and belonging.

There are certain "friends" of ours that we would never even want to contemplate losing. This person gives you what no other friend of yours can. The harsh reality is this: The initial amount of care you have for a person at the start of your friendship with them doesn't always last forever, and you would probably claim to have hundreds of friends if I asked you to give me an accurate estimate. How many are friends, mainly on social media, and how many do you confide in? I strongly encourage you to take time to distinguish those "friends" from the ones who deserve to be your confidants. Now, the list is short. Strive to have God as one in your inner circle of confidants.

You wouldn't describe them using the word "friend." Why? Because your relationship with them is so much more personal that the word "friend" doesn't even come close to describing its true beauty. Instead, you refer to them as "a second dad," "a second sister," or even "a mentor." All of which implies an even stronger relationship than the word "friend" does on its own.

Sometimes it isn't easy to confide in even our closest friends. I know this personally. When I reached the lowest point of my depression and attempted suicide, I did not tell anyone. Not my most intimate friends or any of my family. I kept it to myself. I shared it with God and only God. I leaned on Him heavily during that period. It is because of this closeness and confiding in Him that allowed me to eventually start living stress-free. In my book, *Stress Free Living: Is it possible or just a dream?* I will discuss this in more detail.

We often have a negative mindset when going through tough times, with thoughts running around in our messy minds. It may feel like a heavy weight or a burden on our shoulders. The thoughts take us over, and we find ourselves going where it takes us – which, in most cases, may not always be so pleasant.

In times like this, it is easy to withdraw from others and avoid letting them know what is happening. There is a fear of judgment from others, to let them see the reality of our situation and to face even more negativity. So often, in these situations, we feel alone and isolated. So how do we bring ourselves to the point where we confide in someone about what we are going through?

Like many other processes, this can take stages. Before even getting to the action stage, we must realize a problem. Something is triggering us, and we are not coping well internally. This may play out externally through various actions or coping mechanisms, such as drinking or withdrawing from others. Awareness of our problems paves the way to prepare ourselves to act.

Before any change can occur, having that individual awareness allows us to say we have a problem. We are moving away from the denial and into a space where we are preparing ourselves to address it. The first thought may be, "I need help"; we are not alone in that thought. When we are at that point of needing help, confiding in someone can relieve some of the burdens that we are carrying. While this may be for some people, it may not be for others. At this point, it would be up to us to be true to ourselves and take that step to seek out what is helpful for us. Confiding in God has such a powerful impact on your situation. He knows all about what is on your mind and what help you need and can see endless possibilities of positive outcomes out of any situation. Your closest friends do not have all the abilities God has. I am not suggesting you ignore your closest confidants. God may be using them to help you. I suggest using both avenues.

Allow yourself to be vulnerable. Being vulnerable may seem negative and scary, but it is a positive way to open yourself to a closer and deeper relationship with someone. The vulnerability involves revealing a part of yourself that is hard to talk about but important to share with those your trust and is essential to building a close relationship. Just as you need to be vulnerable with your closest friends, you must be vulnerable with God.

10

Not Just on Sunday

How to grow the relationship

Your relationship with God is the most important relationship you will ever have. It is a relationship that should be nurtured and grown daily. Daily, not just on Sundays. Think of your other strong relationships. Do you designate a single day each week to nurture that relationship? You can do many things to grow your relationship with God that would not just fall on Sunday.

God is always there for us, but sometimes we need extra effort to grow our relationship. Like any relationship, a strong connection with God takes time, energy, and attention. If you want to deepen your relationship with God, here are a few things you can do. Read your Bible regularly. This allows God to speak to you while you pay attention and let you know more about Him and His will in your life. You will be able to hear His voice more clearly. Pray often. We cannot pray too much. This is the most important way to connect with God. Talk to Him about your day, your worries, and your joys. Thank Him for His blessings and ask for His strength during difficult times. Trust me; He will listen. Serve others. This is a great way to show your love for God by helping others.

Try working alongside Jesus. "we are the hands and feet of Jesus" can mean many things. God does not want us all to be a missionary far from home with strangers. But there are things we can do within our church or our community that fulfill His plan. His will. We develop several long-term relationships with co-workers after working alongside them. Let's build our long-term relationship with God by working alongside Him. Be open to what He wants you to do. God does like to stretch us for His purposes. But when we actively seek to further His Kingdom, God will take things we already enjoy and use those to further His Kingdom. So, what is God calling you to help with? Pray about it. Ask God how He would like to use you and ask Him to make it your desire. Maybe it is as simple as greeting you at your church or helping with office work for a Christian non-profit organization.

Do you feel the nudge?

God is with us all the time. He never leaves our side. He has filled us with the Holy Spirit, who guides us along the path of life. But how often do we notice His presence? How often do we hear Him talking to us or feel a nudge in one direction or another? Are we too busy to notice or just not paying attention?

How often have you heard people say, "Just give me a sign," so I know what to do? Or have you prayed for a sign? In the Old Testament, we read about how God spoke.

2 Samuel 22:14 *The LORD thundered from heaven, And the most High uttered his voice.*

1 Kings 19:12 *And after the earthquake a fire; but the Lord was not in the fire: and after the fire a still small voice.*

Psalm 68:33 *To Him who rides upon the highest heavens, which are from ancient times; Behold, He speaks forth with His voice, a mighty voice.*

Has He stopped speaking to us? I do not think this is the case, but we do not recognize His voice. He speaks to our hearts and not to our ears. I was sitting on the balcony at church over 20 years ago and looking over at Gary running the sound board for the praise band during the service. I remember thinking to myself (or so I thought) that learning how to work the board would be neat. That thought quickly went away as the service went on. After the church service, we had our Sunday school class. After class, Gary asked me if I would be interested in learning how to run the soundboard because he could use some help. If anything, it would give him an ocassional Sunday off from working it.

I immediately knew God had listened to my conversation and set up this situation before me. I did not even have to think about whether to pursue soundboard training. I was all in. I do not know if God knew of Gary's needs, put the thought in my head, or heard the idea and nudged Gary to speak to me. I guess it does not matter since it was all God's plan.

God is constantly communicating with us. He puts signs in front of us. There are feelings in our hearts that lead us. He speaks to us through others. Yes, that is what I said. He speaks to us through others. God has communicated in various ways, including angels, His chosen spokesmen (prophets), dreams, visions, miracles, and even through a donkey that He enabled to speak as a man speaks! If you would like to read the whole story of the donkey, you can read about it in Numbers 22. My point is that He is not limited to what our minds can think about His ability to communicate. As we talk to others and share our stories of what God has done in our lives and hear others' stories, God speaks. I know He puts words in my mouth when I converse with others.

Now, you must discern what God is speaking and what is not.

You must know if it is something that is God's will. The more you study the bible, the more you can recognize His "voice" or "nudge". With so many distractions in this world, it gets harder and harder to "hear" Him.

Americans spend more time at their jobs than we do in our homes. What do your actions say to your peers? Colossians 3:23-24 says, "Whatever you do, work at it with all your heart, as working for the Lord, not for human masters, since you know that you will receive an inheritance."

Putting God first is more than starting the day with Him. Having integrity is one way to have Him with you and let others see Him through you. Ethical solid principles always follow integrity. Honesty and trust are central to integrity, as is consistency. Integrity is doing what you say you will and taking responsibility if you cannot accomplish it. For example, if you promise to complete a task by a specific deadline, integrity takes that promise seriously and delivers it on time. Integrity is also accepting responsibility when you do not meet the deadline as promised.

Showing respect to others is a way to have God with you at work. Let Him work through you to determine the best way to treat others. We know what to do, but do we consistently do it? If we know God is with us at work, we will focus more on doing the right thing.

Leading with a servant's attitude is how Jesus would do it. Let Him guide you through this approach at work. Put everyone around you and their needs above yours.

Distractions that make us ignore His presence

We live in a very busy world. Many distractions separate us from God, even if it is just our awareness of His presence. I drive a lot with my full-time job. Often, I will handle phone calls while driving to be more efficient in my day. I do this through the car's speakers and am not holding the phone, but that does not mean it is not a distraction. I may have my GPS system guiding me to my next stop. While on the phone, the GPS software does not vocalize the directions and where to turn next. This forces me to look down at the map regularly as I get closer to my exit on the highway or turn in town. I have had situations where I focus more on the phone conversation and miss my turn.

Now picture that the GPS system is God looking after you and guiding your life. The phone conversation concerns your busy work schedule, toddlers in your house that demand your attention, or financial stress at the front of your mind. We tend to forget about God. He is still there, but we are not aware of Him. We're human, and we tend to be very self-focused. It's easy for us to get lost in our problems and ourselves to the point where we lose sight of God. When we become too focused on ourselves, we no longer focus on God.

Here are other areas of your life where you may find distractions. Your schedule is too full to allow time for prayer. You spend a lot of your day on social media. Some people do not like silence and must always have music playing. Maybe you need some quiet time to "hear" God. What happens if quiet time with God brings up responsibilities you need to fulfill, such as interpersonal reconciliations and job commitments? What if quiet time brings awareness of sin, bad habits, and your need for repentance? Do you avoid quiet time with God?

So, how do you avoid these distractions? As Christians, we must be careful what gets our attention. What fills our minds ultimately fills our hearts. Just because everyone else is doing something does not make it right. Paul reminds us in Romans 12:2 that as Christians we are called to "not be conformed to this age, but be transformed by the renewing of your mind, so that you may discern what is the good, pleasing, and perfect will of God." You must filter what goes on around you to what is important to God. This may mean you must set boundaries to protect us. I have stopped associating with some people that are always negative because I did not want the negative attitudes to influence my thoughts. For example, if you have ever walked a dog, you know they get distracted easily. Whether it is a squirrel, another dog, or anything that moves, you keep them on a leash so they do not put themselves or those around you in harm's way. The constraint is for their own good. Similarly, we must set up constraints and boundaries to protect us.

Turn off the push notifications on your phone. I had to quit using a smartwatch because it reminded me of many things throughout the day that took away my focus on what was in front of me. It drove me nuts to hear a tone for every e-mail, text message, Facebook notification, etc. Limit how much you use social media and how often you check e-mails. Take that free time you just created to build your relationship with God. Be aware of His presence, talk to Him, read your Bible, and look for His plan.

11

9 Habits to put God in the Center of Your Life

We are creatures of habit. The more we do something, the easier it gets; we do not have to try to do it consciously. You can think about it as being on autopilot. It starts early in life. Have you taught toddlers to put on their shoes and tie the strings? They need help initially and must concentrate on the steps necessary to secure the knots. After a while, they do not have to think about it as much; eventually, it comes naturally. That is what we want in our quest to have God at the center of our lives. We want to get to the point where we are flying on autopilot.

Submission

We need to submit to Him fully. Proverbs 3:5-6 says, "Trust in the Lord with all your heart and lean not on your own understanding; in all your ways submit to him, and he will make your paths straight." The heart motivates us to make decisions for our lives, and how we transform it to have sincere faith, we need to submit it to God. Ezekiel 36:26 says *"And I will give you a new heart, and a new spirit I will put within you. And I will remove the heart of stone from your flesh and give you a heart of flesh."* Our egos can get in the way of many things in our lives, but most importantly it prevents us from fully submitting to God.

When you have a significant decision to make, who do you go to for advice? Do you turn to God? He knows what is best for us. We must trust Him completely in every choice we make. That does not mean we disregard our God-given ability to reason, but we should not trust our reason and exclude others. We need to be willing to be corrected by God's word. Bring your decisions to God in prayer; use the Bible as your guide; and follow God's leading as He will direct your paths by directing and protecting you.

Confession

The word "confession" is often misunderstood and misapplied. We think of confession as an uncomfortable person-to-person event – whether before a priest or with a friend we've wronged. If we were to draw a picture of someone confessing, we'd probably draw an embarrassed expression on their face. A YouTube clip would show someone giving scant detail so they, at least technically, weren't lying. Also, they'd look down at the carpet while waiting for the other person to tell them how to make up for what they've done. We must admit our sins, ask for forgiveness, and accept it with gratitude, thanksgiving, and humility. 1 John 1:9 says, *"If we confess our sins, he is faithful and just and will forgive us our sins and purify us from all unrighteousness."* We worship such a merciful God. Confession frees us up to enjoy fellowship with God. It lightens the burden on our conscience. He gives us a clean slate. Confession does not mean asking for forgiveness. God doesn't tell us to ask for forgiveness. When we confess, we can expect forgiveness. God promises. He also promises to cleanse us of all unrighteousness. We no longer must confess our sins of the past repeatedly. That does not mean we should not continually confess our sins since we continue to sin. True confession means we are committed to not performing the same sins again. We would not be genuine if we planned to sin again, thinking we had a free hall pass. Pray for strength to defeat temptation the next time. We must lean on Him for this strength. End your confession with thanksgiving. We have a forgiving God even when we do not deserve it. Thank you, Lord, for your forgiveness.

Study the Word

Remember when you were in school and had to study to learn the topics being taught? You did not just enter the class knowing everything that would be taught, or you may not have signed up for the course. The same principle applies to your goal to be closer to God. We can always learn more as we study more about His Word. *For everything that was written in the past was written to teach us, so that through the endurance taught in the Scriptures and the encouragement they provide we might have hope.* Romans 15:4.

God has provided these teachings for us. We can gain so much knowledge and strength by reading and understanding Scripture. We learn the behaviors that are acceptable to God and what to avoid. We know that even the closest of God's disciples still struggled. It tells us we do not have to be perfect to be loved by God. Even Paul struggled with sin, as depicted in Romans 7:14-15. "So the trouble is not with the law, for it is spiritual and good. The trouble is with me, for I am all too human, a slave to sin. 15 I don't really understand myself, for I want to do what is right, but I don't do it. Instead, I do what I hate."

Do not approach Bible study like reading a textbook and studying for a test. Ask God to speak to you through the words on the pages. Open your heart and mind to understand what He is saying fully. Studying the bible gives you additional insight into how to interpret the message. There are three steps to bible study.

Step 1 is observation. Do you see cross-references to other verses that reinforce the message? Authors in the bible demonstrate that something is important by repeating it. In 1 Corinthians 13, the author uses the word "love" nine times in only 13 verses, communicating that love is the focal point of these 13 verses.

Step 2 is interpreting what you read. Reading the commentary in your bible helps you in this area. Put everything into context. Do not just look at single verses but read the whole paragraph or chapter to understand what the author is trying to communicate. The Bible was written long ago, so we must understand it from the writers' cultural context when interpreting it.

Step 3 is the application of what you read. Application is why we study the Bible. We want our lives to change, obey God, and grow more like Jesus Christ. After we have read a passage and interpreted or understood it to the best of our ability, we must apply it to our lives. How can I apply what I learned to my relationships with others? Does it give me a new perspective on my relationship with God? The application step is not completed by simply answering these questions; the key is putting what God taught you in your study into practice. Although you cannot consciously apply everything you're learning in Bible study at any moment, you can intentionally apply something.

Guidance

People are put into our lives for a reason. They may cross paths momentarily or be there for most of our lives. Use them and their gifts. All of us should have spiritual mentors and try to be spiritual mentors. You may say you do not know how to be a mentor if you now have the depth of faith as the next person. You do not have to be a mentor in the traditional definition of the term. You can lead by example. People see how you treat others. Your interaction with someone you meet in passing or the restaurant's server may significantly impact their day. They may be struggling right now, and your love for how you treat them makes them feel some comfort. The guidance you receive and the guidance you portray factor in bringing you closer to Christ.

Prayer

What are your prayer habits? Do you have a set time each day? Do you have a set routine of what you pray about? I know some people that pray every morning at the same time and others that pray before bed at night. They pray for things that they need, the health of others, thankfulness for the blessings in their lives, etc.

I was reading Matthew 6:7-8 which says, *"And when you pray, do not keep on babbling like pagans, for they think they will be heard because of their many words. Do not be like them, for your Father knows what you need before you ask him."* I then remembered Philippians 4:6, which reminds me to "Be anxious for nothing, but in everything by prayer and supplication, with thanksgiving, let your requests be made known to God." There have still been times that I cannot sleep at night or get any real peace. It is not that I stress over situations, but I am not genuinely giving up my troubles to God.

When I pray for others, I ask God to step in and provide for their needs. He may not give them better health, and He knows they need comfort more than anything. I do not try to box God into a corner of what I feel is best for the situation. He knows firsthand that my decisions have not always been the best solution for me and my issues. Sometimes, I pray longer or about more things. The verse in Matthew tells me that I do not need all those words. I need to open my heart up to the Lord, and He will know what is on my mind and what I need.

I have been dedicating more time to expressing gratitude in my prayers. It is easy to overlook the numerous blessings that surround us and fail to show enough appreciation. Instead of focusing on what we lack, it is important to acknowledge and be grateful for what we already have. Acknowledging and being grateful for what we already have is important for our overall well-being. Instead of constantly focusing on what we lack, shifting our perspective to appreciate what we have can bring us a sense of contentment and gratitude. This mindset helps cultivate positivity and allows us to make the most out of our current circumstances. Gratitude can be practiced in various ways, such as keeping a gratitude journal or simply taking a few moments each day to reflect on what we are thankful for. By doing this, we become more aware of the blessings in our lives, big or small.

Giving God specific requests limits our ability to imagine His possibilities for us. The next few times you pray, just let Him know the situation and ask for His guidance on what the future holds for you and what He needs you to do to follow His will. Trust in His plans instead of getting Him to sign off on ours.

If you trust in His plans, what is there to be anxious about? Nothing. Give it to the Lord. That's why He says to pray; He means for us to tell Him what's burdening our hearts and give it to Him so we can rest. He permits us (and commands us even) to stop thinking about our problems and let Him deal with them. When we do that, He gives us the peace.

Fasting

For thousands of years, biblical fasting has been abstaining from food for spiritual purposes. If you're used to a "three square meals a day routine," going without food as a spiritual practice may sound strange. However, fasting was a widespread religious practice when the Bible was written. Some Christians fast (abstain) from other enjoyable things, whether it is a TV, the internet, or a bad habit. Fasting is a practice of humbling yourself before God. You've missed the point entirely if you're turning a fast into a spiritual ego boost. It is about what is in your heart.

Bill Bright, Cru's co-founder, made it his practice to fast and pray. He believed it played a vital role in what God did through him and Cru as a ministry. He listed several benefits he gained from fasting:

- Fasting is a biblical way to humble yourself in the sight of God indeed. King David said, "I humbled myself with fasting" (Psalm 35:13, New King James Version; see Ezra 8:21).
- Fasting enables the Holy Spirit to reveal your spiritual condition, resulting in brokenness, repentance, and a transformed life.
- Your confidence and faith in God will be strengthened. You will feel mentally, spiritually, and physically refreshed.

It's important to understand that fasting is not a way to get a better response to prayer. Instead, true fasting is a means of fostering a better (humbler) approach to worship.

Service

We are directed to serve Him and others. "Carry each other's burdens, and in this way you will fulfill the law of Christ." Galatians 6:2

We were meant to do life with others. We need the love and care of others as much as others need us in the same ways. Next time you see someone struggling under the weight of a burden, be sure to offer your time, resources, and strength as a blessing to that person. "Share with the Lord's people who are in need. Practice hospitality." Romans 12:13

There is a whole industry of hospitality. It all involves people serving others. This differs from social entertainment, which concentrates much attention on the host. Think about when you have entertained guests and the feeling that your home should be spotless; the food must be well prepared and abundant; the host must appear relaxed and good-natured. Hospitality, on the other hand, focuses on the guests' needs. This could be a space to stay, nourishing food, a listening ear, or acceptance. It is putting others first. This can take place in a messy home. It can happen around a dinner table over a warmed-up can of soup. Don't hesitate to offer hospitality because you are too tired, busy, or wealthy enough to entertain.

Giving

We need to give back to God. In the Old Testament, this would involve doves and goats for sacrifices. We no longer do burnt offerings to God. Jesus, through His sacrifice, took care of that for us. Instead, we give back to Him through others.

We know that when we serve others, we are serving God. In Matthew 25:35-40, we hear:

"For I was hungry and you gave me food, I was thirsty and you gave me drink, a stranger and you welcomed me, naked and you clothed me, ill and you cared for me, in prison and you visited me.' Then the righteous will answer him and say, 'Lord, when did we see you hungry and feed you, or thirsty and give you drink? When did we see you a stranger and welcome you, or naked and clothe you? When did we see you ill or in prison, and visit you?' And the king will say to them in reply, 'Amen, I say to you, whatever you did for one of these least brothers of mine, you did for me'."

What better way to thank God, than in service to Him by service to His children? Consider where you can serve others in your church, work community, family, or neighborhood. Help an elderly neighbor with their trash, help a single mom get her kids to school, serve at your parish's monthly breakfast – and so on. Find the face of Jesus in those you serve. Remember that in serving others, we serve God.

Worship

Plain and straightforward worship is the most direct way to give back to God. Think about it: you give God our time, energy, and presence when you spend time in worship.

Have you heard the phrase, giving lip service? Definition of lip service by Merriam Webster:

: an avowal of advocacy, adherence, or allegiance expressed in words but not backed by deeds —usually used with pay.

I think we, without trying, tend just to give lip service as a form of worship. It is not a matter of just going to church on Sunday and then putting the Bible and our faith on the bookshelf throughout the week. I think this is what Jesus meant in Matthew 15:8–9: *"This people honor me with their lips, but their heart is far from me; in vain do they worship me."*

We need to look at the more public expressions of worship services or daily acts of love, which Paul calls our "spiritual worship"

> *I appeal to you therefore, brothers, by the mercies of God, to present your bodies as a living sacrifice, holy and acceptable to God, which is your spiritual worship.* Romans 12:1. (ESV)

God wants us to offer ourselves, not animals, as living sacrifices. This includes laying aside our desires to follow Him daily, putting all our energy and resources at His disposal, and trusting Him to guide us. This is not in lieu of Sunday worship but complements it. Worshipping with others at church helps build relationships that will strengthen our faith. It also shows us ways that we can serve others.

12

How do You Know it is Working?

Aligning your will with God's will.

Our Father, who art in heaven, hallowed be thy Name, thy kingdom come, thy will be done, on earth as it is in heaven. How often do you say the Lord's prayer? How often do you think about what you are saying? "Thy will be done." Do you want God's will, or do you want God to accept your will as what needs to happen? I pray for all sorts of things. I can honestly say that I am mostly praying for good things. Now I know that not everything in my life has been enjoyable and would not have been something I prayed for, but when looking back, it was part of God's plans. It was His will in my life.

It is a little complicated. How do I pray for God's will when I do not know His will? Philippians 2:13 (NLT) may give us some insight. "For God is working in you, giving you the desire and the power to do what pleases him." God works in and through the obedient. We need Him to work through us because we cannot do it ourselves. We should always be working for and striving to be more like Jesus. God is working "in" us as we are working for that purpose. This does not mean we can sit back and watch God work. We have free will and need to have the desire to fulfill His will. He is working in us, but we need to ensure we do not get in the way because of our free will. It is not God who acts for us. He leads us to do His will, but it is a matter of whether we follow that lead or go out on our own. He does not force us to do anything. If we listen to Him, He will encourage us down the right path. There are two parts to the verse. The first part explains that God is working in us and giving us the desire to do His will. The second part says He will give us the power to do what pleases Him. What pleases Him is His will. God provides us with the ability to do His will. An example of this power is in Luke 10:19, *"I have given you authority to trample on snakes and scorpions and to overcome all the power of the enemy; nothing will harm you."* You may not see snakes and scorpions wandering around you; I know that would freak me out. The symbolical meaning of "serpents and scorpions" is primarily "the works of the devil." He gives us the power to be victorious over Satan. We can defeat the evils of our world through the strength God gives us.

I read this and started to think, "Nothing can harm me," yet I have felt much pain and others against me. But is it really pain and suffering in the overall scheme of things? No. There is no promise that you will love or even like God's will. Some may say you must endure the storm to get to the rainbow. A great example of this is written in the Book of Job.

In this Bible story from the book of Job, a wealthy man named Job resides in an area called Uz with his extended family and vast flocks. He is "blameless" and "upright," constantly mindful to live in an honest manner (Job 1:1). God mentions Job to Satan saying, "There is no one on earth like him; he is blameless and upright, a man who fears God and shuns evil." However, Satan contends that Job is only righteous because God has favored him generously. Satan dares God that, if given the approval to inflict suffering, Job will change and curse God. God permits Satan to abuse Job to experiment with this brazen claim, but he forbids Satan to take Job's life in this manner.

Over the course of a day, Job is given four reports. Each informs him that his sheep, servants, and ten children have all died due to thieves, intruders, or natural disasters. I cannot even fathom going through what he had to endure. And this is a "blameless" and "upright" man that truly followed God. If this happened to Job, what makes me think bad things cannot happen to me? The suffering shows too much for Job, and he turns bitter, anxious, and scared. He deplores the injustice that God lets evil people thrive while he and many other honest people suffer. Job wants to face God and protest but cannot physically find God. He assumes that wisdom is concealed from humans but seeks understanding by fearing God and evading evil. Have you ever asked God, "Why me?" out of frustration? God eventually consoled Job, and Job recognized God's infinite power. Ultimately, Job never gave up hope and faith in God regardless of his situation. Job is an inspiration to us during our suffering.

As the Scripture says, God will give us the desire and the power to do what pleases Him. It took much passion and willpower for Job to continue to have faith in God. God works in our hearts. Have you ever felt drawn to do something good, even though maybe not in your comfort zone? It was God working in your heart. We will have the desire to do God's will.

As He works in us, He transforms our desires to align with His. We need to trust in what He has planned for us. That is not always easy, but it becomes easier as you grow closer to God. Reflecting on your life, you may be more aware of where His plan has taken over your own and where you are better off because He stepped in. Can you think of examples in your life where this has happened? I can name several.

I was very career driven in my 20's and 30's. I was determined to move up the corporate ranks in management, and it cost me money with all the moves around the country and in my relationships because of putting work in front of my family. Finally, I gave control to God in 2008. I prayed that He would direct my career and where I needed to go. That was not an easy thing to do. I like to be in control. Over the years, I have told many people that I make a horrible assistant manager but a great manager. I want to be in control and have difficulty supporting a manager who does not think like me. I have, however, gotten much better about this train of thought over the years. After giving up control to God, I was blessed with an opportunity to transition out of operations management to being part of the accounting team. It was not a position that existed in our company before I said that prayer. It was one of those "wow" moments. You know, the signs from above that we always ask for. Dear Lord, show me a sign so I know you are listening, and show me the way you want me to go. I have continued to grow in this occupational area and have not once, since 2008, strived for a higher-up position within the company. I have been more successful than ever, and it is because of God's will being done. He had much better plans than what I had the desire for on my own. I just had to trust Him and let go of the controls.

Since then, my prayers have changed to include asking for His direction in my life. If I pray for others, I ask God to address their needs. I typically do not pray for their wants. That may come across as cruel. It is if I do not want them to have what would please them. If they are struggling and have voiced what they feel will help them overcome their burdens, I pray that God will give them peace. I hope that their will aligns with God's will. I wouldn't say I like seeing anyone suffer. I want everyone to always be healthy and happy, but that may not be God's plan. Look at the story of Lazarus in John chapter 11. He was very sick, and instead of Jesus immediately coming to heal him, Lazarus passed away. Jesus, a few days later, raised him from the dead. Lazarus' relatives did not ask for his death, but that was God's will. God needed Lazarus to pass away so that Jesus would have the opportunity to perform the miracle of raising him from the dead.

As we pray for God's will to be done on earth as it is in Heaven, we realize it may come with some pain and suffering. In the end, His will is always good. As we grow closer to God, His desires become our desires. Our will starts to align with His will. Over the next week, concentrate on how and what you are praying for. Is it aligning with God's will or our human wants?

I have taken numerous management assessment tests over the years, and they do not change a lot, even though I am becoming a better leader. One thing I see is that I have a judgmental personality. I have tried to be less judgmental over time, but I am making less progress than I would like. Are you aware of your judgmental traits, or do you not have this problem? We also have preconceived notions of what we feel someone would be like before we get to know them.

I was reading a scripture lesson in Acts chapters 10 and 11. Cornelius, a Gentile, had a vision from God telling him to reach out to Peter, a Jew, and hear Peter's message, even though Cornelius did not know what that message was. Around the same time, Peter had a vision giving him insight into the message he would share with Cornelius.

Acts 10:1-8 At Caesarea there was a man named Cornelius, a centurion in what was known as the Italian Regiment. He and all his family were devout and God-fearing; he gave generously to those in need and prayed to God regularly. One day at about three in the afternoon he had a vision. He distinctly saw an angel of God, who came to him and said, "Cornelius!" Cornelius stared at him in fear. "What is it, Lord?" he asked. The angel answered, "Your prayers and gifts to the poor have come up as a memorial offering before God. Now send men to Joppa to bring back a man named Simon who is called Peter. He is staying with Simon the tanner, whose house is by the sea." When the angel who spoke to him had gone, Cornelius called two of his servants and a devout soldier who was one of his attendants. He told them everything that had happened and sent them to Joppa.

Around the same time, Peter had a vision that tested his strict interpretation of Jewish laws. Peter was extremely hungry, and, in the vision, God provided numerous animals for him to eat, but Peter refused, saying they were unclean. In verses 14-15, we read, "Surely not, Lord!" Peter replied. "I have never eaten anything impure or unclean." The voice spoke to him a second time, "Do not call anything impure that God has made clean."

Verses 19-20 While Peter was still thinking about the vision, the Spirit said to him, "Simon, three men are looking for you. So get up and go downstairs. Do not hesitate to go with them, for I have sent them."

I continue to be amazed at how God works in everyone's lives and intertwines them together to perform His will.

Skipping ahead to verses 27-28, While talking with him, Peter went inside and found a large gathering of people. He said to them: "You are well aware that it is against our law for a Jew to associate with or visit a Gentile. But God has shown me that I should not call anyone impure or unclean.

Verse 34-36 Then Peter began to speak: "I now realize how true it is that God does not show favoritism but accepts from every nation the one who fears him and does what is right. You know the message

God sent to the people of Israel, announcing the good news of peace through Jesus Christ, who is Lord of all.

Peter proceeded to tell them about Jesus' ministry, His death on the cross, and resurrection.

Verse 44-48 While Peter was still speaking these words, the Holy Spirit came on all who heard the message. The circumcised believers who had come with Peter were astonished that the gift of the Holy Spirit had been poured out even on Gentiles. For they heard them speaking in tongues and praising God. Then Peter said, "Surely no one can stand in the way of their being baptized with water. They have received the Holy Spirit just as we have." So, he ordered that they be baptized in the name of Jesus Christ. Then they asked Peter to stay with them for a few days.

I was particularly moved by verse 34 when Peter says that God does not show favoritism but accepts all who fear Him and do what is right. How often do we show favoritism? How often are we prejudiced about a group of people who are not like us? This starts early on in our lives and continues through adulthood. Do you remember the one kid in school that did not fit in? Is there someone at work whom people talk about behind their backs? What about those awful people that do not share the same political beliefs as you do? God loves them all! Jesus sought out and hung out with the outcasts who were not accepted by "normal" society. He was creating a model of how to build His church; one lost sheep at a time.

Why do we, as Christians, not adopt this same practice? Look at all the different beliefs about the same God. There are Jews, Catholics, Baptists, Methodists, Pentecostals, and non-denominational organizations, to name a few. How many believe their interpretation is the most accurate and are somewhat intolerant of the others? I do not feel this is what God envisioned when He sent His son to die on the cross for our sins and to offer forgiveness, grace, and eternal life with Him for all who believe in Him. It does not require any action or good deeds on our part, just faith! But if we genuinely believe in Him and what He stood for, how can we be so unforgiving and continue to consider some as outcasts of our society?

Prejudices and favoritism are still prevalent in America. There are those whom some consider impure. We, as Christians, need to stand up and fight against it. But how; I am just one person? You do this through your words and your actions. Do not sit back and condone the unfair treatment of others. Welcome the unwelcome into your group, church, and life, and be the accepting person that Jesus showed us how to be. Jesus showed us how to build His church one lost sheep at a time. Right now, through your thoughts and actions, you may be the lost sheep. Maybe He just found you and wants you to bring the next lost sheep into His flock. Let's celebrate our uniqueness and that God loves us all! Go in peace and find His lost sheep.

Forgiveness – Pay it Forward

Ideally, we reflect on our sins and let them die so that we can have a new life with Christ. We have repented and are forgiven through Jesus dying on the cross. Addressing our sins and asking for forgiveness is only one step God wants us to take. We must also forgive those who have hurt us. That is not an easy thing to do. The actions or words of others have hurt all of us. Perhaps it is a relative who criticized you growing up, a colleague who accused you of something you did not do just so they would not get into trouble, or a spouse who had an affair. Maybe you were physically or emotionally abused, or you had a friend or relative killed by a drunk driver. These wounds can leave you with long-lasting anger, resentment, and maybe even vengeance. Forgiveness means different things to different people. Mainly, however, it involves deciding to let go of the bitterness and thoughts of revenge. We pray that in the Lord's prayer, but do we do an excellent job of it? Most of us do not.

"Pray then like this: Our Father who art in heaven, Hallowed be thy name. Thy kingdom come, Thy will be done, on earth as it is in heaven. Give us this day our daily bread; and forgive us our debts, as we also have forgiven our debtors; and lead us not into temptation, but deliver us from evil."

Matthew 6:9-13

When we do not forgive each other, we carry that burden with us. The other person probably has moved on and is no longer affected by what they did. We continue to harbor anger, frustration, stress, sadness, and many other feelings. When we forgive someone, we can let that action and the associated feelings die and start a new life. Forgiveness doesn't mean forgetting or excusing the harm done to you or making it up to the person causing this harm. Forgiveness can even lead to feelings of understanding, empathy, and compassion for the one who hurt you.

"Get rid of all bitterness, rage and anger, brawling and slander, along with every form of malice. Be kind to one another, tenderhearted, forgiving one another, as God in Christ forgave you."

Ephesians 4:31-32

Why is it that we have such a hard time forgiving someone? Is it because we want justice? We want them to suffer for what they have done. Maybe we want karma to pay a visit. We carry some anger with us because it is unfair that they are forgiven. After all, if we forgive them, it is like we condone their behavior. Forgiving others may seem to be a choice, and in one sense, it is a choice, but God has been very clear about forgiveness. He has given us specific directions in numerous Scriptures, all of which can be summed up in just one word -- forgive!

*And when you stand praying, if you hold anything against anyone, forgive them, so that your Father in heaven may forgive you your sins."

Mark 11:25

Who has hurt you that you have not forgiven? How is it affecting you? What feelings do you have for that person because of it? Pray that God will give you the strength to forgive the person and move forward with your life. Let God work in your life.

Good Samaritans

"By chance a priest came along. But when he saw the man lying there, he crossed to the other side of the road and passed him by. A Temple assistant walked over and looked at him lying there, but he also passed by on the other side. "Then a despised Samaritan came along, and when he saw the man, he felt compassion for him.

Luke 10:31-33 NLT

What thoughts do you have when you read this parable? Does it upset you that people would pass by and not help someone in need? Do you say to yourself, "I would stop"? How often do we pass by someone in need because "someone else" can help them?

Have you seen a cell phone video of a terrible event and wondered why someone was filming instead of stepping in to help? Have you personally witnessed someone being harassed, but you did not intervene? We've all been in a situation when someone talks badly about another person. Do we step in and defend the person? If not, do we ignore the situation or possibly even join in on the negative talk? Why is that? Why don't we get involved? Is it that we are too busy or feel it's not our problem?

In other cases, people risk their lives by pulling someone from a burning car or house. They don't think twice about jumping in to help. What makes them different than the people in the previous scenarios? Jesus' parable talked about the religious men who passed by a person in need but ignored him, while the despised Samaritan was the one who stopped to help. That hits home! As followers of

Christ, we are blessed to learn from His teachings how to love one another.

Jesus came into this world to rescue us. He gave His life for us. That is so powerful! In response to His love and sacrifice, we can love our neighbors and jump in when needed.

There are opportunities all around us. Co-workers who are harassed, talked about behind their backs, down on their luck, and suffering emotionally. We should not just pass by someone who is stranded on the side of the road. We assume they have a phone and can call for assistance, but that may not be the case. People who have lost their homes to natural disasters such as the recent tornadoes in Tennessee. They need enormous amounts of help. What will we do in circumstances such as these?

We can always find a reason for passing by, but now is the time for everyone to step up and be good Samaritans to those around us who are in need.

Servant Leadership

One of the most essential traits is being a servant leader. Jesus taught us that you were strong by being a servant. In the upper room, the disciples were battling over who would have the most power. They were simple men until Jesus came along. They wanted to tap into some of Jesus's influence to benefit their stature in life. Jesus could have just put them in their place. You may have had a boss that has taken this approach a time or two. Jesus' approach was to get down on His knees and wash the feet of the disciples.

It is obvious to us who had the most power in the room. It was Jesus. This symbolic gesture shows us the importance of serving your team. How did it make them feel? They were perplexed. Jesus was teaching them about humility. Humility is a strong trait of a good leader. He was teaching them about serving others instead of expecting them to serve Him. There are several passages in the Bible about the importance of being a servant.

But it is not this way with you, but the one who is the greatest among you must become like the youngest, and the leader like the servant. Luke 22:26

But the greatest among you shall be your servant. Matthew 23:11

We can learn so much from this perspective. Developing our sense of servanthood will take us far in leadership. Carrying that servanthood approach in your leadership style plays a big part in creating a team. So how do you develop this trait?

- Spend as much time or more exploring how you can support your team as you do in setting the expectations you have for them. Are you giving them the tools to be successful? What else can you do for them?
- Have your team evaluate your performance as much as you evaluate theirs. We may think we are doing things right, but are we? Develop an atmosphere that promotes feedback on how you are leading.
- Focus on giving away instead of gaining power. Empower your team to make decisions and impact the path of the group.
- You do not have to have all the answers. Please rely on your team and realize their talents that can complement yours. Some worry their team will overshadow them, so they are no longer needed. Get over yourself. That is self-centered thinking and just the opposite of servanthood.

The fruit of the Spirit is visible in your life

How can you tell the true fruit of the Spirit in your life and those around you? In our modern "don't judge me" culture, it can be difficult to keep ourselves free from compromise and the influence of the world. Everyone has an opinion on what's acceptable, what's trendy, and what's relevant. If we aren't careful, we will find ourselves trying to run our spiritual race on the shifting sands of the world's standards and ever-changing ideas of morality. While we should never judge others for the purpose of condemning them, God does instruct us to judge the fruit in others' lives to ensure that we don't get sucked into following the morality of the world.

"*Watch out for false prophets. They come to you in sheep's clothing, but inwardly they are ferocious wolves. By their fruit you will recognize them. Do people pick grapes from thorn bushes, or figs from thistles? Likewise, every good tree bears good fruit, but a bad tree bears bad fruit. A good tree cannot bear bad fruit, and a bad tree cannot bear good fruit. Every tree that does not bear good fruit is cut down and thrown into the fire. Thus, by their fruit you will recognize them"* Matthew 7:15-20

"By their fruit you will recognize them." We should learn to recognize what is fruit and what is not fruit. Paul breaks it down for us in Galatians:

> "*But the fruit of the Spirit is love, joy, peace, forbearance, kindness, goodness, faithfulness, gentleness and self-control. Against such things there is no law*" Galatians 5:22-23

The fruit of the Spirit is the outward, visible virtues in a Christian's life. They show the presence of the Holy Spirit within us. The opposite of these virtues are the acts of the flesh as also stated in Galatians.

"The acts of the flesh are obvious: sexual immorality, impurity and debauchery; idolatry and witchcraft; hatred, discord, jealousy, fits of rage, selfish ambition, dissensions, factions and envy; drunkenness, orgies, and the like. I warn you, as I did before, that those who live like this will not inherit the kingdom of God" Galatians 5:19-21

As you look at your life, do you see yourself as:

- Being loving to others?
- Being joyful because of what God has done in your life?
- Exuding peace?
- Show patience in difficult circumstances.
- Being kind to others regardless of how they are to you?
- Being a model of goodness?
- Being faithful?
- Being gentle?
- Having self-control?

When you allow God to have complete control

Let go; let God. Have you heard that phrase in the past? Short and simple but oh so tricky. We like being in charge, being in control of our lives. The sovereignty of God refers to the fact that God is in complete control of the universe. A belief in God's sovereignty is distinct from fatalism, which denies human free will. Humans can make genuine choices that have real consequences. God does not directly cause everything to happen, yet He does allow all that happens to occur. And ultimately, God's will is going to be accomplished. These statements may seem unimportant and better suited for an esoteric theological discussion. However, the sovereignty of

God is reasonably practical and has a significant impact on our daily lives. With God in charge, it should remove all cause for worry. So why do we stress about anything? Is it because we do not fully trust Him? Or do we not trust ourselves and the decisions we make on our own?

Romans 8:28 says, *"And we know that in all things God works for the good of those who love him, who have been called according to his purpose."* We can rest in the fact that our God is able to work all things for our good, even when we cannot readily see how that may happen. The sovereignty of God also affects how we make decisions. When we recognize that God is in control, we need not be paralyzed by decision-making. If we make the wrong decision, all is not lost. We can trust God's faithfulness and ability to set us back on the right course. Trust me; He has redirected my course numerous times in my life. On a related note, we can and should make decisions. God's control does not mean we sit idly by and allow life to happen. It means we can go bravely into life, trusting that our loving Father sees the larger picture and faithfully works everything for His glory.

Reflect on your life. Do you recognize where you have been redirected? As I stated earlier, I was redirected when I gave control over my career to God and quit trying to climb the corporate ladder. I was able to start living without stress when I realized He would take care of me. I do not have to solve the world's problems around me. If I let Him control the path and let His will be done, everything will work out how He wants it done compared to my plan. His plan is always better than mine. If you see your stress level going down, it is probably because you are giving up some control of the situation and letting God handle it.

Peace in a storm

I remember a day at work when a new hire was taken around the office to be introduced to everyone. When they got to my office, the person doing the introductions could not remember my new position with the company. I explained that I was the accounting manager but described my role differently. I described my office as the eye of a hurricane. The eye of a hurricane is the center of the storm. Inside the eye of the storm is calm weather and sometimes the sun can be seen. All around it is a wild, strong storm. After I could start living stress-free, I concentrated on providing a stress-free work environment. I told them that if they ever become overwhelmed with everything around them, they should come to my office and discuss it with me. I can calm down the situation. I can provide peace.

What does peace mean to you? Is it relaxation, quieting your mind, and a feeling of tranquility? We use emotional energy to get through the storms of our lives. Anxiety and stress tend to set in when we run out of that energy. We are so used to living with stress and anxiety that we forget there is a better way to live. It is possible to live stress-free. You do not have the ability to get rid of what causes the stress. You must learn how to control how you react to those things.

I am talking about the peace from God within you. It is the presence of the Holy Spirit. A lack of peace comes from a lack of trust in God. Living in peace means we stop our imagination that runs wild with all the negative things that may happen to us. A common saying among Christians today is, "Don't be afraid!", "Fear not!" or variations of this appear in the bible 365 times. I have not found anything that validates this claim of 365 verses. But the philosophy of "fear not" and do not be afraid" is repeated numerous times throughout Scripture. It is important! If we remove this fear from our lives, we can find peace. This is found by trusting God to get us through the storm.

13

Where do we go from here?

Developing a deep and meaningful relationship with God is a journey that requires time, effort, and consistent habits. Just like any other relationship, it requires nurturing, communication, and trust.

One essential aspect of nurturing relationships is confiding in one another. Creating a safe space to share our thoughts and feelings openly is important. Being vulnerable and transparent with those we care about fosters trust and deepens our connection. The same is true with our relationship with God.

However, it's not enough to confide in each other only during difficult times or when faced with challenges. Building healthy habits means making an effort to communicate regularly and intentionally. This means checking in with one another even when things are going well or simply sharing moments of joy together.

When we talk about growing a relationship with God, it is essential to understand the concept of the Fruit of the Spirit. These qualities include love, joy, peace, patience, kindness, goodness, faithfulness, gentleness, and self-control. We can deepen our connection with God by actively cultivating these attributes through prayer and reflection on His teachings.

Furthermore, always confiding in God is crucial for building a strong relationship with Him. We can share our joys and sorrows with Him through prayer or simply talking to Him throughout our day. He longs to be involved in every aspect of our lives - big and small - offering comfort and guidance.

In addition to always confiding in Him, establishing healthy habits plays a significant role in growing our relationship with God. Just as we set aside dedicated time for other important aspects of our lives like work or relationships with loved ones, setting aside regular prayerful meditation or reading sacred texts helps us stay connected to His presence.

Remember that growing a relationship with God is not about perfection but rather progress. It's about embracing imperfections while seeking continuous growth in faith. By focusing on developing the Fruit of the Spirit within us, confiding in Him all the time, and establishing healthy habits, we can foster an intimate bond that sustains us through life's challenges while bringing us closer to His divine love.

May your relationship with God be filled with abundant blessings and continue to flourish and deepen over time.

References

[i] Mere Christianity, Book 4, Chapter 4, "The Good Infection" (1952). Nov 20, 1952

[ii] https://www.newworldencyclopedia.org/entry/Lex_talionis

[iii] https://www.brainyquote.com/quotes/mother_teresa_164917

[iv] https://www.cru.org/us/en/train-and-grow/spiritual-growth/fasting/biblical-fasting.html

[v] https://www.merriam-webster.com/dictionary/lip%20service

Thomas Mayberry is trying to live his life in alignment with what God wants. He struggles, as we all do, but is blessed with a forgiving God. As he has navigated through life, his faith in God has grown. This has allowed him to experience and be aware of even more blessings. Thomas started writing in 2011 to be able to share his story. To witness to others what God has done in his life. It started with his passion for leadership and how his faith guided his leadership style. Out of this came his book, *Faith Guided Leadership*.

He struggled with stress and decided to write a book on the subject. *Stress Free Living, Is it Possible or Just a Dream?* was published in 2013. By writing the book and not hiding behind his stress, Thomas learned how to live stress-free. What God can do for us is amazing when we allow him to step into our lives more.

His third book, *A Marathon Journey, Lessons in Goal Setting*, shows what you can accomplish if you have faith and apply your Christian principles. God sees so much potential in us we cannot even imagine. Earlier this year, Thomas published a devotional for Lent titled *40 Days of Reflection*.

To learn more about Thomas' faithful journey, he regularly posts blogs on his website, https://thomasamayberry.com. You can also check out his author page at https://amazon.com/author/thomasamayberry.

Printed in the USA
CPSIA information can be obtained
at www.ICGtesting.com
LVHW020701240923
758983LV00002B/12